The Getaway Guide IV

The Getaway Guide IV

Short Vacations in Southern California
by Marni and Jake Rankin

Pacific Search Press

Pacific Search Press, 222 Dexter Avenue North,
    Seattle, Washington 98109
© 1983 by Marni and Jake Rankin. All rights reserved
Printed in the United States of America

Designed by Judy Petry

All photographs by the authors except those by the following:
    Lee Krikorian, page 90
    Rancho Las Palmas, pages 116 and 119
    Disneyland Hotel, page 148
    San Diego Visitor's Bureau, page 233
    Hotel del Coronado, page 243

Cover: The boardwalk at Miramar by the Sea

Library of Congress Cataloging in Publication Data

Rankin, Marni.
    The getaway guide IV.
    1. Hotels, taverns, etc.—California, Southern—Directories. 2. Resorts—California, Southern—Directories. 3. California, Southern—Description and travel—Guide-books. I. Rankin, Jake. II. Title.
TX907.R325 1983   647′.979491   82-19060
ISBN 0-914718-77-0 (pbk.)

Wherever you go and whatever you do in the outdoors, move at Nature's pace, seeking not to impose yourself but to lose yourself. If you must leave footprints, make them not with blindness but with care and awareness of the delicate balance around you. And if you must take souvenirs, take them not in your pockets but in your mind and spirit. In preservation lies the promise of renewal.

Pacific Search Press

Contents

The Southern California Getaway

Readers of earlier *Getaway Guides* are well aware of our thesis that to obtain the greatest benefits from the little time off we can take away from our busy daily lives, we should try to divide that time into a number of short getaways scattered throughout the year, rather than spending it all at once in the traditional two-week summer vacation.

We first hypothesized, and have since demonstrated with our own travels, that the first few days of any vacation are by far the most diverting, the best remembered, and therefore the most rewarding. The reason is simply that the initial impact of a change of pace and change of scene distracts the mind completely from ordinary cares and routines by filling it instead with new experiences and pleasant anticipation. Just one or two days of such displacement are extremely therapeutic, so that the mind and spirit are refreshed and afterwards we can return to the old cares with new enthusiasm and new perspective.

Test yourself on your next vacation. If you have gone to a good place and are having fun, the first days when you are happily preoccupied with all that is new and interesting will seem by far the longest and richest. Those are the beneficial days. Spend too much time in one place and, as the novelty wears off, new routines appear, old worries return, and pleasures diminish. In the face of this, we would like to encourage you to try to repeat those first few best days as often as you can to get the greatest benefit from your limited vacation time.

To get these high returns, of course, it is essential to go where you will be comfortable and have pleasant weather, good food, no hassles, and access to the things you like to do. Sometimes you can plan it all ahead, but other times it will be a spur-of-the-moment decision. In either case, the key to making the most of your time is knowing what the possibilities are, where the weather is apt to be good, what activities are available, how long it will take to get there, and how much it will cost.

These are the questions the *Getaway Guides* answer, with descriptions and photographs to help you picture alternative destinations, make your decision, then phone ahead to the numbers listed and make the necessary arrangements.

The previous three *Getaway* books offered trips in British Columbia, Washington, Oregon, and Northern California. This volume, on Southern California, completes our coverage of the West Coast.

We had a good time discovering Southern California. It is a broad, diverse, vibrant area with endless getaway possibilities, so our research to find and get acquainted with the best of them was a challenging, time-consuming operation. We spent many months crisscrossing the lower half of this wonderful state, running down leads, eliminating the resorts that disappointed us, and settling on a selection of the ones that enchanted us enough to fill a diversified, balanced, comprehensive book. These latter we visited one at a time, spending at least a night, but usually two or three. We participated in the activities, ate the food, evaluated the rooms and services, and learned about each getaway's past history and present management philosophy. Our objective was always to discover and chronicle the things readers will want to know to make a selection in the first place, and beyond that, to say enough about each resort so that when you get there you will already know what to expect and what there is to do and can start right off making the most of your available time.

Things can change quickly in the resort business. New facilities are added, old ones are deleted, and management attitudes alter. That makes it necessary to revise and update a book such as this every few years, and to do this we rely on feedback from readers.

We are, therefore, always hoping for and delighted to receive any information you think we ought to have about your own getaways. Notes from you about things you especially liked or didn't like at any of the resorts in this book, or about new places you have discovered that ought to be in it, are one of our most valuable resources.

San Luis Obispo to Ventura
Getaways

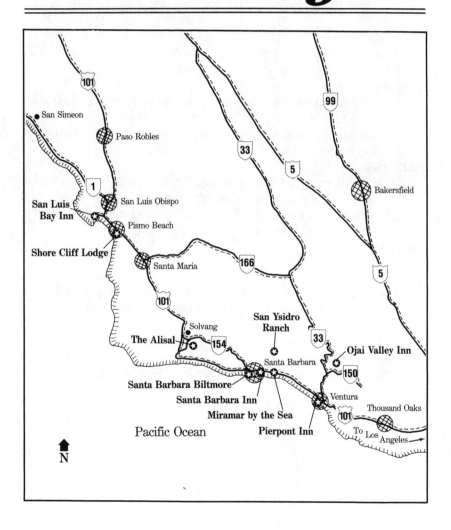

San Luis Bay Inn

Distances:

From Los Angeles—190 miles; allow 3½ hours

From San Francisco—240 miles; allow 4½ hours

Features:

Friendly and attentive service characterize this medium-sized, fully equipped resort; it is located in a small, out-of-the-way community on a stretch of coastline noted for its good, usually fog-free weather

Activities:

Ocean swimming, surfing, and jogging; swimming in heated pool, tennis, golf, deep-sea fishing; historical sight-seeing, and browsing in the shops of picturesque San Luis Obispo; Hearst Castle is one hour away

Seasons:

Year-round

Rates:

$78 for two people for rooms with view of golf course; $94 for two people for rooms with ocean view; suites from $125

Address:

P.O. Box 188, Avila Beach, California 93424

Phone:

(805) 595-2333; toll free in California (800) 592-5928

The San Luis Bay Inn

Like many other noteworthy California properties, the site of San Luis Bay Inn was once a part of a large Spanish-Mexican land grant belonging to the Avilas, a noble family with a history dating back many years. In the late 1700s, the original mission of San Luis Obispo and the town that grew up around it were located about eight miles inland from here, and it was just a matter of time until Port San Luis was built on the bay to provide the mission town with an outlet to the sea.

Today, looking over this crescent-shaped piece of waterfront, you can see the port slightly to the north and the tiny town of Avila Beach to the south, with the San Luis Bay Inn occupying a prominent piece of high ground midway between the two, where it commands a scenic view of the whole sweep of San Luis Bay. A long rock jetty greatly enhances the sheltered waters of the port, which is now home base for a picturesque fleet of commercial fishing rigs, charter boats, and pleasure craft.

Behind and below the inn on the landward side are a warm, shallow tidal lagoon where children like to play and, beyond that, running along two valleys that extend into the green surrounding hills, the inn's eighteen-hole golf course. Below the inn, on the valley floor, are four tennis courts and a driving range. Just to the left, at the head of the entrance driveway, is the clubhouse, a small Spanish-style building that houses an informal bar and sandwich shop for the convenience of golfers and tennis buffs.

The inn itself is an imposing building three stories high, gracefully incorporated into a flower-covered hillside in a manner that mitigates its height and size. Just inside, on the ground level, are the front desk and the elevator foyer, which opens onto a large, welcoming lobby dominated by a fireplace and filled with comfortable furniture and much-used bridge and backgammon tables. In the morning, before the restaurant opens, free "early bird" coffee is set out here, and every afternoon at four it is the gathering place for guests to enjoy a traditional British-style afternoon tea.

To the left of the lobby are the cocktail lounge and restaurant. When the weather is nice, beverages and food can be served out of doors, on an ocean view terrace that opens off the lounge. Beneath the terrace, down a short flight of steps, are an attractive swimming pool and a deck covered with lounge furniture and flanked by vividly colored flower beds.

More important than the physical attributes of the inn, however, are the people who staff it, who have acquired a real knack for making guests feel welcome and at home. Pleasant room furnishings, good food, and attention to detail throughout all contribute to the appealing atmosphere. But the best feature of all is the weather.

San Luis Bay forms a small coastal pocket, uniquely situated so that the sun and prevailing breezes tend to sweep away or burn off the

An old mission on the square of nearby San Luis Obispo

late summer fog by midmorning, when the rest of the coast remains shrouded in gray mists. Avila Beach's boast of three hundred and fifty clear days a year is probably only a slight exaggeration. September, October, November, and December are always sunny. If it rains at all, it will be in January or February, but even then either it rains or it is gorgeous, and on one of those few inclement days you can stay inside by the fireplace and enjoy a game of bridge or read a good book.

Routes and Distances

From the Los Angeles area, drive north on U.S. 101 through Santa Barbara and Santa Maria. After passing Pismo Beach, and eight miles before San Luis Obispo, look for the exit to Avila Beach. Take this exit, and after two miles of winding road you will see the San Luis Inn's golf course on the right, then the village of Avila Beach on the left, and the inn itself on a hillside at the end of the golf course.

From San Francisco and the north, take either U.S. 101 or, if time permits, the more scenic California 1, the Coast Highway, to San Luis Obispo. Continue on past the town for eight more miles to the Avila Beach exit, as above.

Accommodations

San Luis Bay Inn has seventy-four rooms, all of which are spacious and airy, with large private decks for taking advantage of the frequent good weather.

Except for a half-dozen suites, the rooms are all much alike, differing only in outlook, with about half facing the ocean and the others overlooking the golf course and the rolling hills beyond. The rooms are considerably larger than those found in most resorts, and have been furnished with comfortable lounge chairs and useful tables both inside and on the decks. Particularly notable are the very large European-style bath–dressing rooms with sunken tubs that are long enough for luxuriant soaking while you stretch out at full length.

The beds are nicely made up with sheets on both sides of the blanket for a clean, elegant feeling, and while you are out to dinner the maids will turn down the beds and leave chocolate mints on the nightstand. Moreover, the bathroom is picked up at the same time, and any wet towels exchanged for fresh ones, a thoughtful touch that you will particularly appreciate when you have put in a day of tennis and swimming and have run through all the linens.

Activities

With a varied terrain that includes sandy beaches, rolling hills, steep canyons, and a green valley floor traversed by a winding river, the San Luis Bay area is a natural setting for many different sports.

Guests play tennis and golf in back of the inn

Golf is the one that most guests come to pursue, but tennis and water-related activities are also very popular here.

An attractive midweek golf package lures many golfers to try the relatively new eighteen-hole championship course carved into the hills behind the inn. Noted for its great diversity, the course has distinct design differences between the two nines. The front nine snakes through a narrow canyon lined with oak trees that present a hazard to even a slightly errant shot. The back nine is longer and distance takes on more importance as the holes crisscross back and forth over the small river and the place where the tidal lagoon joins the ocean.

Unlike the golf program, which includes a fully equipped pro shop and two resident teaching professionals, tennis at the inn is very low-key. There is no fee for play, and court reservations are unnecessary—guests can use the courts for unlimited periods of time as they are available. Casual as the organization may be, it is no reflection on the quality of the four fine, hard-surfaced courts, which are located in a protected area near the first tee of the golf course, sequestered against onshore breezes and glare from the water.

With a mild climate and good weather just about year-round, swimmers and sunbathers are much in evidence, even in January, lying by the pool at the inn or in the sand on sunny Avila Beach, which is considered one of the safest ocean beaches on the central coast. Joggers have to dodge their way through the bodies when running along the sand, but they have the alternative of quiet roads and trails that lead through the rolling hills in the area. Hikers also have numerous possibilities for roaming without ever leaving the two thousand acres of the property, and nature lovers and bird watchers will be intrigued with the bird and wildlife sanctuary nearby.

So much for onshore activities. For those sport fishermen anxious to put out to sea and try their luck, daily charters depart from Port San Luis, one of the several long, narrow piers extending out into the deep water of San Luis Bay. This is just a few blocks down the road from the inn. Charter boats go out year-round after rock cod and albacore, and also for salmon during the spring and summer runs. From January through April, charters are available for a very different purpose: sighting and observing the whales that pass near the coast.

Inn guests willing to stray farther afield will find many points of interest in the surrounding area. An hour's drive north on Highway 1 will take you to a tour of the incredible splendor of the Hearst Castle at San Simeon. If you travel the same distance in the opposite direction, on Highway 101, you will end up in the quaint Danish village of Solvang. One place you should be sure to visit is the little town of San Luis Obispo, just a few miles north of the inn. It is a small college town with a proud sense of its heritage, and has stubbornly resisted change. It is filled with sights of historic interest, most of them centering around the old mission built in the eighteenth century, the fifth in a string of twenty-one built along the coast by Spanish priests. The parklike plaza surrounding the beautiful old church is the scene of many cultural events, and the fringe of the square is ringed with interesting little shops and restaurants. You can spend a pleasant, enlightening afternoon exploring this area and taking the Heritage Homes walking tour (information is available at the inn).

Dining

The staff of the Bay Inn Restaurant operates on the premise that it is not necessary to be a huge facility to provide first-class food and beverage service, and just about any meal served in the dining room supports that assumption. The excellent cuisine includes Russian, French, and American dishes, and the wine waiter will present you with a list of over four hundred imported and domestic brands, reputed to be the finest wine selection between San Francisco and Los Angeles.

The dining room is an L-shaped area arranged so that every seat has a broad view of the bay or Avila Beach. Even though the room is large and open, subdued overhead lighting supplemented by candles on each table make it warm and intimate.

The service in the dining room is formal, but friendly and efficient. If, for example, you spurn a selection from the list of fine wines and settle, instead, for the house wine, you will find the waiter serves it from a cut glass carafe with the same deft attentiveness that he would his finest vintage. Another nice touch, adding to the pleasure of the dining experience, is the tableside production of many of the dishes. Most salads are skillfully tossed while you watch, and many of the entrées are cooked at your table. Some of the fabulous dessert concoctions, such as flaming cherries jubilee, also make a spectacular show.

Breakfast and lunch are served in the main dining room every day, and on Sunday a champagne brunch featuring a wide variety of quiches, omelets, and crepes is served from 9:45 A.M. until 2:00 P.M. For a more informal lunch after a game of golf or tennis, stop in at the clubhouse for a salad or sandwich.

If you are looking for a dining alternative for either lunch or dinner, the Olde Port Inn, out on the end of Pier 3, the last of the three long docks extending into the bay, is a fun and funky place and a hub of local activity. Downstairs, a bar with loud music and entertainment attracts a constant crowd. The dining area is upstairs in a cozy loft and, with the exception of sirloin steak, all of the menu items are fresh seafood from the fishing boats off Port San Luis. The house specialty is cioppino, a spicy fish stew, and every day the chef's special is posted on a chalkboard. From the windows of this dining room you have a good view of all the activities out on the pier. You can watch fishermen lined up on the edge of the dock patiently tending their lines, and others keeping busy with crab pots, while all around are milling crowds, just strolling and enjoying the scene. It's a lively setting for a good meal.

Shore Cliff Lodge

Distances:
   From Los Angeles—185 miles; allow 3½ hours
   From San Francisco—245 miles; allow 4½ hours
Features:
   Convenient stopping point between Los Angeles and San Francisco on a spectacular ocean bluff; low-key and private, with unobtrusive service and extensive, beautifully kept grounds
Activities:
   Ocean beaches for swimming, surfing, and clamming; tennis, use of heated pool and Jacuzzi spa
Seasons:
   Year-round
Rates:
   $52 to $58 for two people; $8 additional for kitchenette rooms
Address:
   2555 Price Street, Pismo Beach, California 93449
Phone:
   (805) 773-4671

Pismo Beach's Shore Cliff Lodge

The small oceanfront town of Pismo Beach lies roughly midway between San Francisco and Los Angeles and, with a mean temperature of seventy-four degrees and year-round beach weather, it is becoming an increasingly attractive stopover for those who enjoy traveling the coast in a leisurely fashion.

A typical seaside town, with recreation and tourism the main industries, Pismo Beach fronts on a wide expanse of flat sand where the waves roll in and break gently on the shoreline. On the southern extremity of this beach, smooth, rolling dunes attract dune buggy enthusiasts from all around the area. To the north, the coastline changes abruptly and a rugged bluff, with frothy surf pounding relentlessly against its base, rises steeply from the ocean floor.

Shore Cliff Lodge is located on a commanding knoll where the high bluffs begin, from which guests can enjoy a 180-degree view of the ocean, as well as some of the finest sunsets the Pacific has to offer. It is a unique site, and although the lodge was not originally built as a resort, it has assembled all the necessary ingredients for a pleasurable vacation.

The three-story lodge has comfortable rooms, all with ocean views over manicured lawns and colorful flower beds. Several small gazebos built on the extreme extensions of the cliff offer an even better opportunity for viewing distant points—as well as the surf directly below as it breaks over the offshore rocks before churning into hidden coves and rocky tidepools.

Finally, an inviting swimming pool and Jacuzzi are tucked between two wings of the lodge, where they are protected from the wind but have a fine view. Fifty yards further along the cliff's edge in a separate building are the restaurant, and beyond that, the lodge's two tennis courts at the extreme end of the property.

All in all, Shore Cliff is a complete resort complex and a handy getaway spot for enjoying a quiet retreat.

Routes and Distances

Pismo Beach is a long, straggly town ten miles south of San Luis Obispo, squeezed between U.S. 101 and the Pacific Ocean. Shore Cliff Lodge is at the northern tip of town where it borders on Pismo's twin village, Shell Beach.

From the south, as you come up 101, look for the Shore Cliff sign, clearly visible on the left, and almost immediately thereafter look for and take the Shell Beach exit. This exit goes under the highway and emerges onto a frontage road (Price Street) that parallels the highway. Go south again for several hundred yards and you will see the lodge on the right.

From the north, after passing Shell Beach, get off the highway at the well-marked Price Street exit. The exit ends almost directly in front of the lodge.

Accommodations

There are times you may want a lot of personal attention, and there are times you would prefer to be left alone to do things your own way without pressure of persuasion. When the latter mood prevails, Shore Cliff is your kind of place. Here, you check in at the front desk and are immediately on your own to park your car, carry in your luggage, fetch ice if you need it, and decide your own schedule. The lodge runs with a minimum of "out front" personnel; but you will immediately see many signs that plenty of attention is paid behind the scenes—the premises are kept scrupulously clean and neat, for example, and maintenance of the lawns and flower beds is meticulous.

There are an even hundred rooms, all comfortable, and each with an ocean view, its own private balcony, and roominess and furnishings that invite guests to lounge and relax. Every room has a color television, equipped with remote control.

At Shore Cliff, upper level rooms are considered more desirable, since each floor up offers that much better a view, so prices are slightly higher for the second floor and higher again for the third. All rooms are alike, except for eight efficiency units that have kitchenettes com-

Individual balconies face the Pacific sunsets

plete with refrigerators, small stoves, toasters, coffee makers, and all necessary utensils. Ice machines are available on each floor, and self-service elevators provide access to the upper levels.

Activities

Go to Shore Cliff Lodge when you want to take it easy and relax—the whole layout is conducive to leisure. The little gazebos on the cliff over the ocean invite you to sit and quietly read or converse or, perhaps, watch the activities to the south at Pismo Beach. The flower-bordered swimming pool area that faces west to catch the sun all day offers another pleasant place for lounging or, for more privacy, you can sit on your own little balcony.

If, nevertheless, you feel an urge to get some exercise, the lodge provides two tennis courts at the north end of the property, free for guests, on a first-come, first-served basis. The court surfaces are good and there are lights for night play. These are "view" tennis courts, set at the edge of the cliff above the ocean, so there may occasionally be the inconvenience of wind or—the bane of late summer in these parts—morning fog. The entrance to the courts is kept locked, so guests must pick up the key at the front desk whenever they wish to play.

Although you can look down on the long sweep of Pismo Beach from the lodge, actually getting to it requires driving south on Price

The Shore Cliff's private ocean beach

Street into the village of Pismo Beach and then right several blocks to the waterfront. This beach is a favorite surfer's hangout and the parking lots are peppered with Volkswagen beetles with boards strapped on top. Commercial activity in the town caters to these casually dressed young people, with a predominance of small beer parlors, electronic-game arcades, short-order and Mexican food purveyors, and inexpensive motels.

On the beach itself, you will always see surfers working the waves, picnickers spreading their blankets, waders and swimmers testing the water, and joggers running up and down. Far to the south, where the dunes begin, it is just possible to see the brightly colored tents where dune buggy aficianados camp to pursue their sport. And, anywhere along the wide sweep of beach at any time of year, you will usually see clam diggers with their shovels and buckets out working the low tides.

Lodge guests who want to enjoy the beach with a bit of exclusivity have a tiny cove at the base of the cliff all to themselves. It is reached by descending a high spiral staircase located between the restaurant and the tennis courts. Surf casters like this spot, too, but more often the fishermen go a few miles to Port San Luis where they can arrange charters for deep-sea fishing, or try for rock cod and bottom fish off the long pier. Freshwater fishermen go inland to Lopez Lake, which offers good trout fishing and has a small marina where rowboats and tackle and bait can be rented.

Any visit to this area would be incomplete without a short trip to explore San Luis Obispo. Most of the things worth seeing are accessible on foot: park near the town square that contains the old mission and start from there. Literature available at the lodge describes all the points of interest to look for.

Dining

The Shore Cliff Restaurant is under the same management as the lodge, but it is located in a separate building just a short stroll away on the same spectacular bluff. It is open 365 days a year, serving guests breakfast, lunch, and dinner, and the operation might well be characterized as good food, moderate prices, and a priceless view.

For breakfast, anything is available from a simple continental coffee and roll to the fanciest omelet. Salads and sandwiches dominate the luncheon menu, and for dinner there is a choice of chicken, chops, steak from the broiler, and a variety of fresh seafoods.

Whatever fare is chosen, the enjoyment will be enhanced by the sight and sound of the surf pounding on the beach below. You can time your meal to coincide with one of the spectacular sunsets off of Pismo Beach, and when dusk comes, dramatic floodlights illuminate the waves.

There is entertainment in the bar every night except Monday, and it is pleasant to linger a while after dinner, have a nightcap, listen to the music, and perhaps join the others on the dance floor.

Another restaurant, just a few blocks away at Shell Beach, has a solid reputation for fun, revelry, and great food. This is F. McLintocks Saloon and Dining House, which has an old-time western atmosphere and a staff that feeds customers as if they were hungry cowpokes right off the range. Before dinner, however, spend a little time in the saloon, because here you will enjoy the environment of a bygone time. Antlers, stuffed deerheads, old-fashioned pictures, and other early western memorabilia are mounted on the walls surrounding the big circular bar, and a guitarist perched on a stool in the corner by a friendly fire keeps the place lively banging out familiar tunes. Take advantage of this last chance to whet your appetite, because you're certainly going to need a good one. From the moment your waitress seats you in the midst of the bustle of the informal dining room, the food starts coming. First, a basket of fried onion rings, piping hot, while you study the menu. Then, no matter which entrée you choose, you will be served a spinach salad with hot dressing, baked beans, salsa sauce, cottage potatoes, and hot bread. Portions of everything are generous—if you order a steak, for example, you will find when it arrives that it is at least 2½ inches thick.

At just about the point when you wonder if you will survive such bountiful fare, your waitress will appear once more and offer you dessert or a choice of any one of sixteen liqueurs, on the house. What to do? Relax, order a cup of coffee to sip with it, and sit back and enjoy the unusual hospitality of this fine restaurant.

The Alisal

Distances:

From Los Angeles—132 miles; allow 2¾ hours
From San Francisco—297 miles; allow 6 hours

Features:

An old, established ranch resort, notable for its low-key, friendly
atmosphere in a first-class setting; the Santa Ynez Valley
offers captivating scenery, mild, smog-free weather, and a
wide range of things to do

Activities:

Golf, tennis, horseback riding, swimming, Jacuzzi spa, sailing,
fishing, badminton, and other lawn games; use of recreation
room and library

Seasons:

Year-round; April through November is the busiest season and
always popular with golfers; June through Labor Day are
very much family-oriented

Rates:

Tariff for summer and weekends year-round is $160 to $185 per
day for two people; two-day minimum stay; all rates modified
American Plan (including breakfast and dinner); special midweek packages in fall, winter, and spring including golf,
tennis, riding, and meals, range from $240 to $275 per person
for 4 days, 3 nights; 12 percent added to all bills to cover
gratuities

Address:

P.O. Box 26, Solvang, California 93463

Phone:

(805) 688-6411

The Santa Ynez Mountains frame The Alisal's bungalows

When Alisal was established in 1936 as a cattle ranch, it seemed quite natural that it should derive its rather romantic-sounding name from the Spanish word for sycamore, since rows of these huge trees lined the banks of the little creek running through the property. Today the ranch comprises ten thousand acres of valley land along the creek, as well as the high rolling hills on both sides, all flanked by the rugged Santa Ynez mountain range to the south.

In the early days, the old ranch was primarily devoted to running cattle, but 350 acres along the creek were set aside for guest facilities that operated as a sideline during the summer months. Thanks to the beauty of the area and its generally mild weather—with over three hundred sunny days a year and cool, pleasant evenings—these facilities prospered, and were improved and enlarged. So what began as a rustic, limited operation gradually added a golf course, tennis courts, a swimming pool, and many new cottages, until the atmosphere of rusticity became one of quiet refinement.

Riding is still a favorite activity and the ranch stables maintain a large string of fine horses, but today more people probably come for the golf and tennis and just to lounge around the big pool—happier to look at the scenic beauty of the surrounding hills than to ride out into them. Whatever their reason for coming, the management reports that some 80 percent of their guests have been to the Alisal previously—an enviable statistic in the fickle resort industry. The ranch has people who come regularly two or three times a year, and others who have checked in annually for twenty years in a row. One couple has celebrated Easter here for twenty-seven years!

The reasons they keep coming back vary with the individuals, but most feel something personal about the Alisal experience that they are anxious to recapture. Much of the help has been with the operation a long time and maintain a tradition of amicability that is infectious; new arrivals find themselves saying "hello," falling into conversation, and finally making friends with other guests naturally and easily.

The people who come in the summer with their children like it that the ranch provides counselors and activity programs for the youngsters that keep them busy and happy, leaving the adults free to pursue their own activities. Finally, everyone seems to appreciate the American Plan payment system, the package plans that make it possible to predict all costs in advance, and the inclusion of a gratuity in the final bill, which makes it unnecessary to tip during the stay.

Routes and Distances

The Alisal is located two miles south of the picturesque Danish town of Solvang, in the heart of the Santa Ynez Valley. To get to Solvang, first drive north on U.S. 101 from Santa Barbara to Buellton (or south on 101 from San Luis Obispo). At Buellton, turn east on State Route 246. Raising thoroughbred horses is a major activity in this part of the country, and on the short drive between Buellton and Solvang you will pass a dozen or so beautifully kept and often well-known stud ranches. At Solvang, proceed straight through to the Alisal Road at the far side of town. Turn right and go two miles past the golf course to the Alisal Guest Ranch sign at the entrance.

Accommodations

All of the guest quarters on the ranch are in groups of bungalows built around several big quadrangles of lush, green lawn. The cabins on one of these quads are called Golfers Row, because they are separated from the fairways of the golf club only by Alisal Creek. Another central group of bungalows surrounds a huge expanse of lawn with a swimming pool and Jacuzzi in the center, and a third cluster faces the dining hall across a lawn dotted with oak and sycamore trees. Finally, the entrance drive to the ranch is lined with a row of larger three- and four-bedroom cottages for groups and large families.

There are sixty-three units in the compound, all within easy strolling distance of each other, the dining room, and the various centers of activity. With ten thousand acres on which to spread out, and with the extreme popularity of the ranch, it would seem feasible and logical to expand, but such is not the thinking of the long-time owners. To them, small is beautiful, and they want to keep the Alisal just as it is.

As the Alisal rate schedule indicates, there are two basic prices (not counting the large, multibedroom cottages) and two types of accommodations. The difference between them is that the more expensive bungalows have a separate bedroom and 1½ baths. These also have studio couches in their large living rooms, which can be made into beds and thus accommodate two more guests. In most plans, the master bedroom is in a loft, with either a king bed or twins, and has a full bath opening off of it. The half-bath is on the lower level, just off the living room.

The smaller, less expensive bungalows are generally the older units. These have an even larger living room, furnished with twin studio couches that convert to beds, and a spacious dressing area that holds a third studio couch, suitable for a child to sleep on.

All of the cottages are comfortable, though simply furnished. Each one has a log-burning fireplace, which is much appreciated since even during the warm summer months evening breezes from the mountains can cool things off quickly. There are easy chairs by the fireside, in addition to the studio couches, and enough space in the big living rooms to entertain other guests or set up a bridge game.

Other attractive features of the bungalows include covered porches with comfortable lounge furniture, and parking conveniently arranged so that guests can keep their cars near their cottages unobtrusively. The absence of televisions and telephones from the units adds to the restful atmosphere, but for those who don't want to miss a favorite program, there are televisions in the library and recreation room.

Activities

So many activities go on year-round at the Alisal that it is hard to know which ones take precedence. This is especially true in the summer, a time when the ranch becomes very family-oriented. Twice a day, the wrangler saddles up the string of horses and conducts two-hour trail rides into the rolling hills and around the perimeter of lovely Lake Alisal. At about the same time as the early ride, golfers are headed for the first tee of the Alisal's eighteen-hole course, and tennis buffs start migrating to the cluster of seven courts around the tiny pro shop.

The ranch's big swimming pool and hot spa are centrally located in an expansive green lawn, ringed with giant oaks and sycamores. Many guests come for a dip after some other rigorous exercise, or for a soak in the Jacuzzi to ease sore muscles, but it's no disgrace to laze around the pool all day reading and relaxing—and many do.

The flat grass areas around the cottages are settings for badmin-

Guests ride throughout the ranch's 10,000 acres

ton, volleyball, and other lawn games, while a horseshoe pit on the perimeter of the lawn and an archery range just beyond that fill the air with the sounds of clinking horseshoes and whizzing arrows.

In the summer months Lake Alisal, about three miles into the hills from the ranch house, becomes a popular spot. A station wagon is always available to carry guests to this privately owned lake, where some like to try their luck fishing for bass and bluegill, which they can do either from the shore or from one of the rowboats kept for that purpose. Others take advantage of the fleet of eight-foot sailboats also tied up at the pier for learning to sail or exploring the lake. It is also delightful just to drift lazily on the water, taking in the beautiful scenery; and, from some vantage points, if you look up into the mountain peaks you can easily spot a green meadow that belongs to Alisal's distinguished neighbors, Ronald and Nancy Reagan.

One of the most popular summer activities is an early morning breakfast ride every Wednesday to an old adobe shelter up in the hills. Here breakfast is cooked out in the open and the wrangler regales guests with stories of the old days in these parts. It seems that over the years the relaxed atmosphere and pleasant surroundings of the ranch have made it a favorite of many motion picture personalities. He loves to recall the day Clark Gable and Lady Sylvia Ashley were married at the ranch, and how Burt Lancaster, on a rare rainy day, took all of the children into the recreation room and, grouping them around a big fire, enchanted them with stories for a couple of hours.

Another special event is the regular Saturday night steak fry, a big favorite with everyone. A local band plays old-time western music to liven up the barbecue, and following dinner the party moves inside for old-fashioned square dancing with a professional caller.

It is easy to see what keeps the joint jumping in the summer, but even though the pace changes come fall, from then through spring is the favorite time for many, especially the golfers. During this period, some very attractive midweek packages are offered in which room rates are reduced and which include golf, tennis, and horseback riding.

A year-round event is the wine-tasting party held every Tuesday evening between 6:30 and 7:30 in the Oak Room Lounge. The ranch staff serves complimentary samples from some thirty local wineries. It is a pleasant time for newly arrived guests, who can mingle and get to know one another while they nibble cheese and compare these new and little-known vintages.

With so much going on at the ranch, it is hard to find time for side trips, but all guests should try to spend a few hours exploring nearby Solvang, an authentic Danish village filled with fascinating shops and restaurants, and quite representative of a flourishing local Danish culture.

Dining

Dining at the Alisal is so sumptuous and convenient as to convince anyone who is not already convinced that the modified American Plan, properly executed, can contribute to the pleasure and relaxation of a vacation.

All guests are assigned their own tables with name cards on arrival and keep the same table throughout their stay. Breakfast and dinner are served in the warm, friendly ambience of the rustic Ranch Room. The floor is covered by a hand-hooked rug, and a big freestanding brick fireplace—usually aglow—fills the center space of the room. The informally set tables are each adorned with an arrangement of fresh flowers and the tables along the windows look out over the lawn through the branches of ancient oaks and sycamores.

Breakfast is served any time between 8:00 and 9:45. Guests drift into the dining room at their leisure, pick up a complimentary newspaper, and sit down to a piping hot cup of coffee while they decide whether to have the bountiful buffet breakfast or order from the menu. The buffet is almost irresistible, with its selection of fresh fruits, including melons, strawberries, figs, and grapes, as well as a choice of scrambled eggs, bacon, ham, sausage, hot cakes, chicken livers with mushrooms, crepes, and English muffins. It is necessary to

The Danish community of Solvang is just to the south

remind yourself that you are going to eat again that day, because it all looks so good.

Guests are on their own for lunch. They can have it in the Sycamore Room, which is a separate restaurant on the ranch maintained for the general public, or they can have a bite at the snack bar in the golf clubhouse. Lunchtime is also a good chance to try the specialty dishes and Danish pastries in the numerous restaurants and cafés in nearby Solvang.

The dinner hour once again finds Alisal guests at their appointed spot in the big dining room. Often couples who come to the ranch alone find congenial friends, and the management is happy to rearrange tables in order pair them up.

Dinner is served anytime between 6:30 and 8:00 and, after a soup and salad course, guests can choose among five entrées. Prime rib is always on the menu, as are a fish selection and a vegetarian dish. The other two selections change each day. The desserts are excellent, and all of the baked goods are made in Solvang expressly for the ranch.

A pleasant way to cap off the evening is to stop in next door at the Oak Room and listen to some good live music while enjoying an after-dinner drink.

Santa Barbara Biltmore

Distances:

From Los Angeles—92 miles; allow 1½ to 2 hours

From San Francisco—334 miles; allow 7 to 8 hours

Features:

An old, well-known resort hotel on spacious grounds fronting Santa Barbara's famous ocean beach; recently purchased and now operated by the Marriott chain; the grounds and buildings are handsomely maintained and the services extensive and elegant

Activities:

Swimming in heated pool, access to ocean beach, use of adjoining Beach Club's Olympic pool and diving facilities, a variety of lawn games, and complimentary bicycles; golf and tennis available nearby, shopping and sightseeing just three miles away in Santa Barbara

Seasons:

Year-round

Rates:

$110 to $175 for two people; suites and two- and three-bedroom cottages at correspondingly higher prices

Address:

1260 Channel Drive, Santa Barbara, California 93108

Phone:

(805) 969-2261; toll free (800) 228-9290

The Santa Barbara Biltmore—one of "the grand hotels"

The Santa Barbara Biltmore is invariably mentioned on any list of America's finest old hotels. In his book *The Grand Hotels,* J. J. Kramer includes it as one of only nineteen of the nation's venerable inns he considers to be deserving of the title.

It seems every successful resort hotel that has survived and maintained its reputation and popularity over the years has a central theme or spirit around which it organizes its energies and management emphasis, and which establishes the special character by which people know it. The Biltmore, having stood on its beach-front site since 1927, has consolidated its image and reputation exactly in the Grand Hotel tradition. It is known as a place to go for those seeking a touch of old-world charm characterized by elegance and formality and where great emphasis is placed on attentive personal service. If you want things to be perfect and are willing to pay for it, the Biltmore is for you.

The perfection extends beyond the hotel itself: located in the Montecito section of Santa Barbara, the Biltmore is in the heart of a community with one of the strictest building codes in the country. No billboards, garish commercial signs, or high-rise buildings mar its picturebook loveliness. Everything built here must be approved by a strict Board of Architecture, which favors low, rambling structures in the California mission style. This accounts for the overwhelming preponderance of homes and commercial buildings with white or cream stucco exteriors and red tile roofs set on well-maintained grounds. The net result of this restrictive planning is a community that is a restful treat to eyes jaded by the ugliness of urban sprawl. The Biltmore, with its buildings widely spaced on twenty-one acres, fits right in with this concept, and indeed, because it has been admired for so long, perhaps its examples helped establish the Board's criteria.

As if to emphasize the beauty of the hotel's low, white structures, nature has studded the grounds with tall, dramatic cypress and palm trees and rimmed the entire complex with the rugged Santa Ynez range. In front of the hotel, to complete the picture, is the broad Pacific, with the faint outline of the Channel Islands usually visible through the ocean haze.

Finally, for all of its beauty and other attributes, the hotel's reputation is helped no small amount by the reliably mild climate and clean air for which Santa Barbara is renowned, with the average maximum temperature year-round of seventy-two degrees.

Routes and Distances

The hotel is no more than a quarter-mile from U.S. 101 at the southerly end of Santa Barbara. Driving in either direction on 101, look for the exit to Olive Mill Road. Take the exit, head toward the ocean on Olive Mill, and you will soon come to a sweeping right turn that will put you on Channel Drive. The Biltmore is the group of white, red-roofed buildings you see immediately on your right, set well back on a wide lawn.

Accommodations

It is interesting to try to define just what it is that distinguishes really fine hotel accommodations from ordinary ones. Certainly spaciousness is important, and comfortable, tasteful furnishings and decor mean a lot. But the crucial factors are service and attention to detail. When your every need and desire seem to have been anticipated, you know you are in the hands of a skilled professional staff, and this is exactly what the Biltmore strives to furnish.

Most hotel rooms, suites, and cottages here are spacious. A hotel room in one of the main buildings is typically furnished with two extra-long double beds, an armoire, and two comfortable easy chairs with a table and a good reading lamp between. There is also a dressing area with a large walk-in closet and a chest of drawers.

The more expensive rooms have ocean views, and sometimes have larger sitting areas than the less expensive ones.

The cottages are scattered all about the grounds, under palm trees, and are surrounded by lawns. Each can be rented as a complete

Stucco cottages are scattered over the grounds

house, with living room and attached bedrooms, or can be divided by closing soundproof connecting doors. The individual bedrooms are similar to the hotel rooms. The studio units (actually the living room of a suite) have fireplaces, and the bed is a pullout sofa.

As for amenities, each accommodation has an attractive armoire concealing a television set (which is on the cable with Home Box Office programming), a small refrigerator unit containing an ample ice supply, and a writing desk. In the bathrooms you will find an assortment of some things you might have forgotten: shampoo, a shower cap, bath salts, a sewing kit, a shoeshine cloth, and a bag for soiled clothes. When you return from the beach and are dismayed to find tar on your feet, you will even find specially treated towelettes to remove it. And in the evening, while you are at dinner, a maid will turn down your bed for the night.

Activities

Santa Barbara is famous for three things: its weather, its long, wide beaches, and the profusion of handsome Mediterranean architecture, all of which add to its reputation as America's Riviera. Guests at the Biltmore are well situated to enjoy these features. The beach is easily accessible directly across Channel Drive from the hotel. At low tide, joggers and walkers have at least three miles in either direction to run or explore, and for nine months out of the year they can stop for an ocean swim at almost any point in pleasantly temperate water. Meanwhile, all along the route they can admire the shoreside architecture, ranging from elaborate estates and condominiums to a long row, at the southern end of the beach, of close-packed, funky and imaginative little beach houses close to the water's edge.

The inn's regular pool, centrally located among the cottages, is enclosed by a low wall to moderate wayward breezes. It is a favorite gathering place, more convenient to the rooms than the elaborate beach club, and used more for casual lounging in the sun than for serious swimming. An attendant provides a stack of towels, making it unnecessary to bring towels from the rooms.

Just across the drive, the Coral Casino Beach and Cabana Club is a delightful place to spend the whole day. This is a private beach club that extends membership privileges to hotel guests. Your room key is your pass to get by the front desk. You must arrive in street clothes and will be assigned a locker, for a fee of four dollars, to use for the day. The beach club has an Olympic-size pool with high diving platforms. There are also an outdoor hydrotherapy pool, a sandwich bar, and a cocktail lounge with a pass-through window to provide service on the pool deck.

A spacious lawn back at the inn itself is set up for lawn games, including a pickleball court, a permanent croquet course, four shuffleboard courts, and an eighteen-hole putting green. In addition, complimentary bicycles available from the bell captain provide an ideal way to get around and see the immediate neighborhood.

In the hotel lobby, a concierge maintains a desk for the specific purpose of giving people ideas about things to do in the area and then making the necessary arrangements to do them. She can arrange starting times and transportation to three nearby golf clubs at which the hotel maintains memberships, and to the Miramar Club for tennis and paddle ball. The most popular request between February and April is for the whale-watching trips emanating from the Santa Barbara marina. Three boatloads a day go out for 2½-hour searches and, we are told, almost invariably sight whales, sometimes a lot of them.

The concierge also will plan driving trips with marked area maps to follow, noting highlights to look for, and will outline walking trips through the old historic section of Santa Barbara. Additionally, she can send you up to San Ysidro Ranch or to the Gene O'Hagan Stables for horseback riding and help with just about any special requests hotel guests might make.

Dining

Dinner is traditionally a formal affair at the Biltmore, and men are

Sunday brunch outdoors at the Biltmore

expected to wear ties and jackets. Continental cuisine is served every evening in leisurely fashion in the quiet elegance of the La Marina dining room, with piano music providing background. The menu is well balanced, with a variety of dishes to tempt the palate, and the service is deft and attentive. Some of the highlights we recall include an excellent Chardonnay served as the house wine in lovely crystal decanters, an outstanding Caesar salad expertly prepared tableside, and an irresistible cart of pastries wheeled by at dessert time.

In the summer months, beginning on the Memorial Day weekend, a seafood buffet is set up on the La Marina Patio to offer an informal outdoor dining alternative. It includes a bountiful salad bar and meat selections, as well as the choice seafood.

The meal in which the Biltmore takes the greatest pride, however, is the Sunday brunch, which, believe it or not, must be limited to six hundred people and usually turns many away. It is a most elaborate affair, with the buffet set up in the dining room, an elegant array of food amid fountains and ice sculptures, and cooking stations ready to prepare special omelets and other dishes to order. Once guests have served themselves, they take seats on the terrace, where champagne flows freely and gay music is provided by a lively trio that plays to the constantly full house from 10 A.M. until 2 P.M.

The Coral Casino Beach Club, across the street from the hotel, offers another convenient dining possibility. Every Thursday, Friday, and Saturday evening there is dinner dancing there in the main dining room, and luncheon is served Wednesday through Saturday. The Beach Club also has a popular snack bar, The Raft, where swimmers and sunbathers can pick up a sandwich or salad in their informal garb.

Santa Barbara has so many interesting restaurants it is hard to make recommendations, but a favorite spot for lunch on a sunny day is the lovely fountain courtyard of the Presidio Café. It is on Anacopa Street in the heart of Old Town and, after taking the "Red Tile Tour" of this historic area, the Presidio courtyard is the perfect stopping point, where you can rest under a colorful umbrella and sip a glass of wine while enjoying one of the crepe or quiche specialties of the house.

If you should happen to be looking for a dinner spot in town on a Thursday, Friday, or Saturday night and like real French cooking, stop by Mousse Odile, a tiny sidewalk restaurant on Cota Street, just off Anacopa. This is where the natives go to enjoy a delightful meal of seafood, pepper steak, or a variety of lamb dishes cooked the way only the French can. For a description of other restaurants in the Santa Barbara area, check the chapters on Miramar by the Sea and the Santa Barbara Inn.

Santa Barbara Inn

Distances:
From Los Angeles—92 miles; allow 1½ to 2 hours
From San Francisco—334 miles; allow 7 to 8 hours

Features:
A long-established inn facing Santa Barbara's famous beach, and close to Stearn's Wharf and downtown attractions; features Don the Beachcomber's Restaurant

Activities:
All beach activities, including surfing, swimming, walking, and jogging; heated pool and whirlpool spa on premises; municipal tennis courts and public golf courses nearby; bicycle and wind-surfer rentals available at the beach

Seasons:
Inn operates year-round, with June, July, August, early September, and all weekends considered "high season"

Rates:
$72 to $120 for two people, depending on season, time of week, and whether room has an ocean view or mountain view

Address:
Cabrillo at Milpas Street, P.O. Box 4187, Santa Barbara, California 93103

Phone:
(805) 966-2285

The Santa Barbara Inn on Cabrillo Boulevard

All week long the broad beach just across Cabrillo Boulevard from the Santa Barbara Inn provides a promenade for joggers, roller skaters, bicyclists, picnickers, and casual strollers. It makes a busy scene, but nothing compared to Sundays, when it seems that a good part of the population turns out to cheer on a multitude of volleyball and frisbee contests and to see an impromptu mile-long arts and crafts fair that colorfully materializes along the boulevard, all clearly visible from the balconies of the inn.

Santa Barbara is known as a lively place, full of things to see and do, and it is the inn's central location, close in to the points of interest, that helps account for its reputation as a good place to stay in the area. Another part of the appeal is the inn's relative nearness to the big urban centers to the south. The prevailing good weather completes the picture. With the high, dramatic Santa Ynez range rising directly behind town to form a weather barrier on one side, and the even temperature of the ocean acting as a moderating influence on the other, the long coastal strip between seldom experiences temperature extremes, and smog is unknown. Of course, Santa Barbara does have its winter, when it can rain hard, but this is confined mainly to January and February, and even then there are clear periods between showers. The rest of the year the sun usually shines, and the average high and low temperatures for the whole year seldom vary more than twenty degrees.

The inn itself has long been a landmark because of its prominent position on the beach and the popularity among Californians of its Don the Beachcomber Restaurant. You can spend a morning at the beach, an afternoon exploring the old mission and the town, and then watch the Pacific display one of its brilliant sunsets while you linger over dinner at a window table in the restaurant. Not a bad getaway if you've been spending too much time in the big city's concrete jungles.

Routes and Distances

In Santa Barbara, Cabrillo Boulevard, which parallels U.S. 101, runs the length of the broad, heavily used East Beach. The inn, approximately halfway along this stretch at Milpas Street, is impossible to miss from either direction. Those coming from Los Angeles and the south on U.S. 101 can turn left to leave the highway at the Milpas intersection. From there it is just three blocks to Cabrillo Boulevard and the inn.

From the north, turn right off the highway at Chapala, Anacapa, or Santa Barbara Street to Cabrillo, then go left along the beach until you see the inn.

Accommodations

With the exception of a few suites, all of the rooms in the inn are basically the same size and have identical floor plans. Each is furnished with either a king, a queen, or two double beds, with no variation in price due to the kind of bed. The rate range is based solely on three factors: the season, the day of the week, and the view. Fridays and Saturdays are always ten dollars more per room than weekdays; the summer season—that is, June through Labor Day—is ten dollars more than the rest of the year; and ocean view rooms are ten dollars higher than the ones on the mountain view side. It is that simple.

The units are all moderately spacious, well lighted, and quite comfortable. Each has a small dressing area with a sink and vanity and a bath with an extra-large tiled stall shower. Large, fluffy towels and an extra telephone complete the luxuries here.

The rooms are furnished with a matching table and wicker chairs, plenty of lamps, a digital clock and radio on the bedside tables, and complimentary Home Box Office television. A spacious, comfortable deck is furnished with two chairs, a chaise lounge, and a coffee table.

In the evening, a maid turns town the beds and leaves a little present—mints and fresh fruit to enjoy before retiring—and in the morning a complimentary copy of the *Los Angeles Times* will be found outside your door. Room service from Don the Beachcomber is quick and reasonably priced.

Small boat moorage near the inn

Activities

The inn has an attractive swimming pool with a hot whirlpool spa alongside, both positioned to catch the sun throughout most of the day. You can swim there, or cross Cabrillo Boulevard and swim in the ocean, then come back to the pool to rinse off. Or, you can spend the whole day on the beach. Walkers will enjoy going the mile to Stearn's Wharf, either along the beach on the hard part of the sand at the water's edge or on the bike path bordering the outside edge of the beach. The section below the wharf is known as East Beach and beyond the wharf is West Beach. Go out on the wharf to look at the shops and the fishermen who frequent its far end. Then continue along West Beach until you come to the harbor and small boat moorage. This is another absorbing place to saunter about for an hour or two, especially around five o'clock, when the commercial fishermen are returning from a day at sea. The boats and the people are colorful— you can see the crews breaking out beer and gesticulating and shouting from boat to boat, explaining their luck and exchanging greetings. There are snack bars, tackle shops, chandleries, boat sales docks, and charter-fishing piers, and never any end to interesting character studies to catch the eye.

It should be stressed that this is a big harbor and one of California's busiest. Commercial fishing, after tourism and oil production, is probably Santa Barbara's most important industry. The shelter afforded by the Channel Islands makes it an ideal area for sailing, too, so the harbor is loaded with many fine pleasure craft to observe, as well as the commercial boats.

If ever you have entertained the thought of learning wind-surfing, this might be an opportunity to take a fling at it. A little enterprise with the name of Sundance Windsurfing maintains a school at the far end of West Beach, easy to locate because the gaudy sails of its tiny craft are much in evidence out on the water front. They will rent you a wind-surfer for ten dollars an hour, and if you want instruction, provide that for twenty dollars for two hours, including all equipment. It generally takes about six hours of instruction and practice to get the hang of handling these tricky and exciting little sailboats.

Whale watching is another maritime experience many people enjoy during the season, November through April. Trips leave from the Sea Landing dock at the marina—ask at the front desk for details. A little publication, "This Week in Santa Barbara," is also available at the front desk and is useful for newcomers to the area. The centerfold usually features a good map that pinpoints most of the major attractions in town. There is also a list of places to eat, along with information about goings-on in general, as well as any special attractions. Most visitors take the twelve-block "Red Tile" walking tour through the Presidio, El Paseo, and old section of town.

To play tennis, go about a half-mile out around the end of the bird refuge lagoon on Cabrillo and back a short way on Coast Village Road to the Santa Barbara municipal tennis courts. This is a big complex with more than a dozen courts, including night lighting, that are free to players on a first-come, first-served basis. Evenings are the most popular time, but you can usually walk right onto a court during other hours.

For golfers, the inn has golfing privileges at several nearby courses and can explain the details and make arrangements on your behalf. Ask about this at the front desk.

Dining

When traveling it is undeniably a convenience to have a first-class restaurant at the place where you stay, and the Santa Barbara Inn fulfills this admirably with Don the Beachcomber's practically down the hall from your room.

Not only is it convenient, but Don the Beachcomber's is a real treat for anyone with a predilection for Polynesian food. The chain has been operating in the South Pacific since 1934 and today has a string of restaurants throughout the western states, all very similar in appearance. The Santa Barbara Inn provides an especially pretty setting for the typical Polynesian decor. Its octagonal seating arrange-

Lunch outdoors at the Presidio in old Santa Barbara

ment, with a circle of windows looking through palm trees out to the ocean, makes a pretty good substitute for an island in the South Seas.

This restaurant has always been known for its big selection of exotic drinks, but there are also just as many interesting items on the dinner menu. The specialty of the house is called the Early Bird Polynesian Buffet, served from 5 P.M. until 8 P.M., Sunday through Thursday. You can choose from a marvelous variety of dishes including carved roast beef, Cantonese pork, chicken with mushrooms, Szechuan shrimp, rice, an assortment of vegetables, salad ingredients, and another assortment of desserts. Surprisingly, it is one of the most reasonably priced dinners you will find in Santa Barbara. Live piano or organ music and the agreeable decor contribute to making this a pleasant way to spend an evening.

If you are staying several days at the inn, you will want a little variety and, though there are a great many options, Stearn's Wharf is so close you ought to try one of the seafood houses out on the pier. The long-time favorite is the Harbor House, which burned eight years ago and has been recently rebuilt; it is fast recapturing its original good reputation. It has a fine seafood menu and posts a daily list of specials from the East Coast, the gulf coast, and the West Coast on a big blackboard by the door.

Farther out on the wharf is Moby Dick's, which is a bit more infor-

mal and less expensive than the Harbor House and enjoys wide popularity. You can eat out on a sort of enclosed porch that has a fine view
of the whole Santa Barbara harbor. Regular dinner selections are
available and also a variety of short orders such as fish and chips and
fried shrimp in a basket.

Santa Barbara is loaded with good places to eat, so these two on
the wharf are just for starters. See the chapters on The Miramar and
The Santa Barbara Biltmore for a few additional suggestions.

Miramar by the Sea

Distances:

From Los Angeles—92 miles; allow 1½ to 2 hours

From San Francisco—343 miles; allow 7 hours

From downtown Santa Barbara—4 miles

Features:

A big, old, well-kept resort on the ocean, attractively landscaped with subtropical plantings; there are many diversions, and the prices are reasonable

Activities:

Sunning, sitting, and jogging on the wide sand beach; tennis, paddle ball, swimming in two heated pools, Jacuzzi, complete men's and women's exercise rooms, saunas, and miscellaneous lawn games

Seasons:

Year-round

Rates:

The price range goes all the way from $32 to $86 per night for two people, with an average around $50; suites and cottages suitable for families are also available

Address:

P.O. Box M, Santa Barbara, California 93102

Phone:

(805) 969-2203; toll free in California (800) 322-6983; toll free outside California (800) 241-3848

New lanai rooms surround a second swimming pool

It would be hard to find anyone who travels much on U.S. 101 through the Santa Barbara area who is not familiar with the bright blue rooftops on the cluster of white cottages and buildings that mark the Miramar Resort complex. This roadside landmark has been distinguished by its colorful roofs since 1940, but the history of the resort dates back much further to 1877, as attested by the collection of nostalgic memorabilia in the lobby. A glass showcase contains registries from bygone days, some of them opened to show the entries of a parade of prominent visitors from the early 1900s on. There are pictures on the wall showing the resort as it looked in those days, many newspaper clippings, and—most fascinating of all—some old menus, including one from as recently as 1959, when the most expensive dinner was listed at $2.95!

The history of the Miramar began when a farmer named Daulton started taking in guests when times were hard. The picturesque setting, tucked in between a beautiful, protected stretch of oceanfront and the Santa Ynez Mountains, combined with the salubrious climate, made this a much more profitable business than farming. Cottages were built to handle the overflow of guests who began flocking to the area. As time went on and the Miramar gained a worldwide reputation, the famous and wealthy came by yacht and in their private railroad cars. To accommodate the latter, the Miramar even had its own

The Southern Pacific line stopped at the inn in the 1880s

station, which still stands on the property. It is interesting to note that when the Southern Pacific line was cut through in the 1880s, Doulton was very proud that he was able to divert the route so that it avoided his cornfields and ran instead down near the "worthless" beach. At about the same time, a pier five hundred feet long was extended into the ocean for the pleasure of those who wished to tie up and spend a few days at the Miramar, and kings, queens, and presidents— including Theodore Roosevelt and Woodrow Wilson—were among this illustrious group.

In its more than a century of existence, the Miramar has been owned and managed by only two families: in 1939 the Gawzers took over from the Daultons and are still running it today. Many changes have taken place during the last forty years. One hundred and fifty new rooms have been added, as well as two swimming pools, a Jacuzzi, exercise rooms, and a delightful seaside boardwalk built from the wood of the old pier when it was eventually torn down. The development of fifteen acres of meticulously maintained gardens filled with exotic subtropical plantings and colorful flowers especially enhances the present charm of the resort.

Most important, however, of all of the Miramar's fine attributes are its five hundred feet of private beach in a protected cove that is safe for swimming and playing in the surf, making it the only hotel in the area that is directly on the oceanfront. Southern Pacific trains still whistle through the property several times a day close to the rooms lining the beach, but guests don't seem to mind—in fact, they rather enjoy the excitement and nostalgic memories the railroad brings, while their children run out, as they always have, to watch and to wave at the engineers.

Routes and Distances

Coming from either direction, at approximately four miles south of Santa Barbara look for exits from U.S. 101 to the San Ysidro Road. Coming from the south, you will cross over the freeway on the San Ysidro Road and immediately turn left into the Miramar entrance road. From the north, drive straight ahead from the exit ramp into the Miramar entrance. Look for a profusion of bright blue roofs, the Miramar trademark, easily seen from the freeway in either direction.

Accommodations

Because of the unique zoning code in the Montecito area of Santa Barbara, resorts are required to build at least 80 percent of their accommodations cottage-style. This, plus the fact that the Miramar expanded gradually over a period of many years, helps account for the diversity of the two hundred guest rooms and suites at the resort.

The first units to be built were the individual little white cottages dotted around the central portion of the property. These have a distinct personality and each is named Honeysuckle, Cherokee, and so on. One of the most centrally located, just across from the tennis courts, has been turned into the tennis club office, while another is used for a beauty shop. The rest are still favorite quarters for guests, who have the choice of renting just a single room or taking a whole cottage, which includes a cozy parlor with a fireplace and kitchenette and anywhere from one to three bedrooms. These cottages are comfortably furnished, have nice porches, and are right in the heart of the activity. The individual rooms, if taken separately, are the least expensive accommodations in the resort.

Another group of units, designated poolside rooms, are just south of the main building where the offices, gift shop, and dining room are housed. These rooms are in a two-story, U-shaped structure built around a large swimming pool and Jacuzzi. The units are typical hotel-type rooms, comfortable and pleasantly appointed. The ones on the upper level are furnished with two double beds, and the units below have one double and a single. These are reasonably priced, on the lower end of the rate scale.

The lanai rooms are scattered in the lush garden and lawn setting on the north side of the property, with many overlooking a second swimming pool. These units, furnished with two double beds, are newer and considerably more spacious than those previously described, and are somewhat higher priced. Each one has a sliding glass door out to a private deck or patio.

At the top of the scale are the boardwalk rooms. These are two-level units, almost identical to the lanai rooms in floor plan and furnishings, but they face and open onto the long, broad boardwalk that runs the entire length of the five hundred feet of oceanfront. Every room enjoys the sight and sound of waves breaking on the warm, sandy beach right at its doorstep.

Activities

Miramar's beach is fine yellow sand with a firm base and a long, gentle slope into the water, making it particularly suitable for swimming and jogging. As it does everywhere, the tide brings in seaweed and debris, but what makes Miramar's beach especially nice is that every morning the hotel's crew turns out with rakes and shovels to completely clean the beach for the comfort of the guests. Later, when the day warms up, guests flock down to lie on the sand, or to sit along the boardwalk and watch the activity. There are always surfboarders out on the waves to watch, sometimes wind-surfers and children flying kites, and always a parade of people strolling up and down. Often in the morning you can see a seal or two fishing in the shallows, and always a variety of seabirds winging by.

The beach is Miramar's outstanding attraction, and everybody seems to find a way to enjoy it. Those who play tennis will find the Miramar courts easy to reach and good to play on. The hotel has a full tennis program headed up by a tennis director and pro, Hilbert Lee, who has taught for many years in the Santa Barbara area, long a center of tennis activity. There are four good courts, each one individually fenced and screened, all located right in the center of the hotel compound. Next to them is a smaller paddle ball court. All play is arranged by reservation at the tennis shop, and there is a charge of $5 per court hour ($1.25 each, for example, for doubles players).

Other activities on the premises include use of the two swimming pools, one of which is equipped for diving, and a big hot spa which is reserved for adults only (guests eighteen or over). Next to the tennis shop are two elaborate exercise rooms and saunas, one for men and one for women, and both full of shiny Universal gym equipment that is reflected in the mirrored walls. The services of a masseur or masseuse are also available in each gym area. Use of the exercise rooms is $3 and massages are $25 per hour.

A couple of outdoor ping-pong tables, a shuffleboard court, and children's playground equipment complete the activities list, except

Lunch at the dining car

for the not-so-active but extremely popular sport of watching the trains rolling past the little Miramar station. For things to do in nearby Santa Barbara, you might refer to the Santa Barbara Inn chapter in this book.

Dining

For breakfast, some people like to have room service deliver a tray to one of the tables on the boardwalk, where they can eat at leisure in the early sunshine and watch the day get under way on the beach.

One pleasant place for lunch is the nostalgic, authentic dining car parked on a siding next to the old Miramar Station and overlooking the tennis courts. There you can get sandwiches, salads, ice cream, and beer and wine, either to carry to one of the colorful umbrella tables on the veranda at the end of the diner, or to eat inside just as if you were on one of the trains that rumbles by every so often.

Breakfast and lunch are also served in the main dining room, of course, which is no more than seventy-five yards from the boardwalk. It is an attractive garden room, full of rows of potted ferns, trees, and palms that serve as dividers, with hanging ferns cascading from the ceiling. Skylights brighten the room and give it an arboretum appearance in the daytime; at night it is made intimate by candlelight.

The dinner menu in the dining room has a long list of regular entrées, plus a shorter list of daily specials, so there are many items from which to choose. Soup and salad accompany dinner and the prices range quite widely, like the menu itself, so it is possible to eat very reasonably if you wish. Whatever you choose, you can expect good food, attractively presented.

If you should be staying several days at the Miramar and want to sample a different dining atmosphere, it is only minutes into Santa Barbara, where a person could eat out every night for a month without going to the same restaurant twice. Two of these places worth trying, both rich in atmosphere, are located within a block of each other on State Street in the old-town section, three blocks east of the highway. One of these is Maggie McFly's, decorated in "Old San Francisco" style to the nth degree. It is informal, with a bar as big as the dining room usually packed with young people having a good time. Before you make a final decision about the best salad bar in California, you must try Maggie McFly's.

The second spot is the Head of the Wolf, a seafood and steak restaurant in the building that once housed the oldest drugstore in Southern California. It, too, has a popular bar, formerly the soda fountain. Interior walls of sandblasted brick, the original hexagonal floor tiles, and dark woodwork complete the old-time decor.

At the opposite end of the scale for price, demeanor, and pace is the very elegant French restaurant, La Chaumière, at 1305 State Street; the food is expensive, but superb. In between these extremes is the popular Castagnola's Lobster House on Cabrillo, opposite Stearn's Wharf, where for years people have been content to line up and wait their turn for the "freshest seafood in town." The restaurants on Stearn's Wharf itself are replete with nautical atmosphere, and it is pleasant to stroll up and down the wharf and read the menus posted outside before picking the place you want to eat.

San Ysidro Ranch

Distances:

    From Los Angeles—100 miles; allow 2 hours

    From San Francisco—350 miles; allow 7 to 8 hours

Features:

    San Ysidro is the ultimate getaway; nestled against the Santa Ynez Mountains behind Santa Barbara, in an area where fine weather is the rule, it offers seclusion, exclusivity, attentive service, and comfort

Activities:

    Tennis, heated pool, horseback riding, hiking trails into the mountains

Seasons:

    Year-round

Rates:

    Cottage rooms range from $98 to $119 for two people; suites are from $149 to $189, and cottages with private spas from $239 for one night

Address:

    900 San Ysidro Lane, Montecito, California 93108

Phone:

    (805) 969-5046

The San Ysidro Ranch has served guests for 90 years

The San Ysidro Ranch has enjoyed a reputation as a premier resort for ninety years, and those who visit the ranch today are treated to the same rustic elegance, privacy, and low-key ambience that has continued to attract discriminating guests over time.

Thirty-eight secluded cottages, each one different from the others, are scattered on a hillside sheltered by the Santa Ynez Mountains behind and looking westward over the broad Pacific. If you stay here, you may be in the same cottage where Sinclair Lewis or Somerset Maugham or Winston Churchill wrote one of their works, or where John F. Kennedy and his bride came to honeymoon, or where any one of dozens of Hollywood stars came over the years to unwind and relax in private.

It is often difficult to put your finger on the subtle appeal that sets some places definitely apart from all the others, but whatever it is, San Ysidro Ranch has it. For thirty years Ronald Colman was the ranch's owner, and since he understood the needs of his Hollywood associates, he set an operating tone under which they could feel secure and comfortable. When he died in 1958, the property went into bankruptcy, temporarily ending its glorious days. It languished for some years, until it was bought in 1976 by Susie and Jim Lavenson, old hands at the hotel business, who set about to recapture those essential intangible qualities so important to Ronald Colman. "People who come here want to return to a tradition," explain the Lavensons, who completely refurbished every one of the cottages and common buildings in a way that recaptures the spirit of the past. The efforts included stripping their own New York home of many beautiful furnishings, as well as hunting far and wide for additional antiques and fine pieces of furniture and decorations. The taste is impeccable in every cottage, but each is distinguished by its own whimsical elements that bring a smile when you come across them unexpectedly.

Over the years, the ranch has achieved an atmosphere that is an unusual blend of casualness and formality. During the daytime the former prevails. If guests feel like socializing, for example, they drift into the Hacienda Lounge in whatever garb they have on to watch a program on the ranch's only television set or chat with each other. Hot coffee and tea are always available here, and guests can mix themselves a drink from the "honor bar," where they write out their own tabs.

In the evening, however, traditions are upheld and—typical of the gentle humor that prevails—you will note a small reminder in your room advising that the two rules of the house are that gentlemen will please wear jackets for dinner and remove their spurs before retiring.

Routes and Distances

There is no problem finding the San Ysidro Ranch. Everything in the area is named San Ysidro, and the ranch is more or less the apex—located as far back into the mountains as the district goes.

From U.S. 101, look for the San Ysidro Road exit a very short distance east of Santa Barbara. Go north on San Ysidro Road, past Montecito Village to San Ysidro Lane, and turn right. Follow the lane, which winds through some very posh residential neighborhoods, to the entrance to the ranch. That is all there is to it.

Accommodations

The theory at the ranch is that if you happen to hanker for steak and eggs and a Bloody Mary on your own patio for breakfast, you've got it. Unbelievable, but true. There are 110 employees on the payroll to take care of 38 cottages, and they are there for one thing—to make sure that guests are perfectly comfortable.

No two of the cottages are alike—some are very old, some brand-new, and you need a map to find a few of them. But all are flawlessly maintained: a top management team makes a weekly inspection, item by item, of every room on the place to supplement the regular staff's daily maintenance.

All rentals are by advance reservation, of course, and when you arrive at your cottage you will find your name in large letters hanging below the name of the cottage.

Due to the very wide range of prices and attributes, you should decide approximately what type of accommodation you want before you call to make a reservation. The least expensive cottage room, for example, is a bedroom-sitting room in elegant country inn style. There is always some kind of outside foyer or deck, and all rooms are beautifully furnished in the Lavenson's special style. Next on the scale is essentially the same arrangement, but somewhat larger, and with a

The cottages have private decks, some with a hot tub

fireplace (and plenty of wood). Then come the suites, which have separate bedrooms and living rooms. Finally, there are complete cottages, which are little individual houses.

No two of these accommodations are alike. Most, but not all, have fireplaces. (One, Rose, has two fireplaces!) Eight of them have private Jacuzzis or hot tubs, some have complete kitchens or kitchenettes, a few have wet bars, some have large private terraces or decks, some just the very small foyer but lawn chairs out in front. Make a decision about all these factors and the price you want to pay, then call reservations and try to reach a compromise on what suits you best. It might take a visit or two to settle on the one you like most, which may explain why half of the ranch's customers are repeat business.

It will be encouraging to people who can't leave home without Fido to know that the ranch's rate sheet lists "well-behaved pets at $5 a night—European Plan." It also lists "horses stabled, $17 per night, American Plan (gourmet hay)," so that horses apparently have a better deal than either dogs or people, who have to pay for their own food.

Activities

Like all else at San Ysidro, the activity is low-key, and you can be sure no one will blow a bugle in the morning to tell you to get up and get at it. Relaxing and absorbing the beauty of the surroundings and the salubrious climate are quite enough for many.

There are a number of interesting things to do for those who want to be up and about. A bird's-eye view of the ranch would reveal three fine hard-surface tennis courts, for example, an inviting pool, and a stable with a string of saddled horses munching hay out in front.

The three tennis courts are set on the uppermost level of the ranch's developed property, with nothing beyond them but woods and mountains. Unfortunately for tennis players, the high location provides beguiling views out over the Pacific and up to the Santa Ynez peaks, making it difficult to keep an eye on the ball.

The ranch's heated pool is located close to the tennis courts, so it too enjoys the fine views. Angled to catch the sun's last rays, it occupies a pleasant garden setting, with plenty of towels always conveniently supplied on the spot. Barbecue lunch and bar service are available poolside on most weekends and other times of especially active use.

Despite the name, San Ysidro is no longer a working ranch, and only the horses remain as a reminder that it once was. Four one-hour trail rides are conducted each day into the foothills. These are easy rides with gentle mounts, always taken at a walking pace tailored to first-timers and inexperienced riders, but an excellent way to enjoy some more of the area's scenic canyon and distant ocean views.

A more strenuous and popular way to enjoy the same scenery is to

Guests ride and hike in the Santa Ynez foothills

set out on foot over the network of hiking trails that start from the stables area and lead back among the 540 acres of the ranch's own property and well beyond, into the Los Padres National Forest. The most popular hike starts along the bridle trail that follows San Ysidro Creek and continues for 4½ miles up to one of the Santa Ynez peaks. Other routes will take you to a pretty waterfall or a natural hot spring deep in the woods. The office will provide a trail map to take along that will help you find your way home, and the Plow and Angel will provide box lunches if you decide to make a day of it.

Dining

Some guests at the ranch disappear into their cottages on arrival and aren't seen again until departure time. When you take into account that many cottages have completely private decks, their own hot tubs, fireplaces, wet bars and refrigerators, it is quite understandable. But the practice leads to a joke posted in the lobby: "If a guest doesn't come out of the cottage for twenty-four hours, we do force-feeding." Instead of "forcing" guests, however, the ranch provides a room service menu for all three meals that is identical with the regular menu in the dining room, except that no prices are shown— you're not supposed to worry about that.

At any rate, whether you eat on your private deck, in front of the fire, or in the dining room, the fare is acknowledged to be among the best in Santa Barbara. The menu is not extensive: one chicken item, two veal, two beef, two lamb, and the nightly chef's specials, which usually include seafood. But each item is always impeccably prepared, garnished, and served, and there are usually many people from town eating in the dining room—a good measure of the restaurant's quality. If you can't decide which entrée to choose, try the sautéed Wisconsin veal with two sauces and you won't be disappointed.

The dining room, called the Plow and Angel (ask your waitress to tell you the name's story), is friendly and intimate and has an outdoor deck for fine weather. At one time, when the ranch was a ranch, this was the fruit packing room. Downstairs, what is now the piano bar was once the wine cellar. Some things never change.

Dinners are priced at the high end of the scale and everything is à la carte, so the salad, appetizers, desserts, and so on are extra. After you have tried and appreciated this elegant fare, for a complete change of pace the next night, take your jacket off, leave your spurs on, and go up to the Cold Springs Tavern at San Marcos Pass for dinner. The drive, which takes about thirty minutes, is something you ought to do anyway, just for the scenery. The tavern is 118 years old and looks it. From the outside it resembles a group of little board shacks, all alone in the woods with nothing else around for miles. You enter into the bar, which has a big stone fireplace, deer heads and old hunting pictures in profusion all over the walls, and brass spittoons on the floor. The burly, hail-fellow-well-met proprietor is usually on duty as bartender. There is a tree growing through the wall back of the bar, and batwing doors provide entry to the dining room. The food is good, an experience not to miss, and by averaging the cost with one of your dinners at the ranch you will come out about the same as if you had eaten at a regular restaurant downtown. To get to Cold Springs Tavern, drive west on U.S. 101 to the outskirts of Santa Barbara where California 154 to San Marcos Pass branches to the right. Go all the way to the top of the pass, and one mile beyond look for Stage-coach Road to the left. Go one mile on Stagecoach Road and look for the tavern on the left. A call ahead for reservations would not be out of order.

Ojai Valley Inn

Distances:
   From Los Angeles—75 miles; allow 1½ hours
   From San Francisco—372 miles; allow 7½ hours
Features:
   Ojai enjoys a well-deserved reputation as one of the nation's
   premier golf resorts; a beautiful setting, reliably moderate
   weather, and gracious facilities and service characterize this
   old-line inn
Activities:
   Golf, tennis, horseback riding, swimming in heated pool, lawn
   croquet, Friday and Saturday evening dancing, children's
   playground
Seasons:
   Year-round; prime season is ten months, March through December;
   January and February constitute the Ojai Valley's short, mild
   winter
Rates:
   $115 to $175 for two people on the full American Plan, which includes all meals; midweek packages of three days and two
   nights, which include all golf and tennis fees, are $280 for two
Address:
   Ojai, California 93023
Phones:
   (805) 646-5511; in Los Angeles (213) 388-1151; in San Francisco
   (415) 434-0660; in Seattle (206) 682-1981

The front entrance to the Ojai Valley Inn

The Ojai Valley Inn perches on the crown of a hill at the highest point in the Ojai Valley, where it looks out in all directions across a green, meticulously groomed golf course to the surrounding foothills of the Sierra Madres. Of the many things the inn and the area it occupies have in their favor, the unusually fine climate occupies a high place on the list. January and February will have some rainy days, but even then the winter temperature averages between sixty and eighty-five degrees. The rest of the year, "summer," it averages between seventy and ninety, and if the days get hot, the dry air keeps them from being unpleasant, and the evenings are always cool.

The now venerable inn was founded over fifty years ago by a wealthy easterner searching for a place to settle that would aid his delicate health. The moderate climate and shelter from fog and dampness provided by encircling mountains made Ojai Valley seem to him the perfect spot.

In addition to being a healthy atmosphere, the good weather makes it possible to pursue many sports year-round, prompting the easterner to build a small golf course and the modest original inn to provide room for friends and visitors. The building was rambling adobe with a sprawling red tile roof, and that part has not been changed. Ojai's ten-month "high season" and its proximity to Los Angeles attracted golfers, and its reputation began to build.

When the present general manager, William Briggs, took over in the mid-1950s, the development of the inn accelerated. He expanded the golf course to eighteen beautiful, challenging holes. The main building was enlarged, cottages were built on the hillside, and the dining room upgraded to offer the finest cuisine. The final step was the construction of a complete new tennis center.

Continuity of management and an experienced staff have given this inn's operation a professionalism that insures that whatever needs doing gets done quietly, on time, and with seeming ease. The result, from the visitor's point of view, is friendly, skilled, unobtrusive service that conveys a sense of welcome and hospitality. You can't help but like Ojai and quickly feel at home, which puts you in a mood to enjoy everything it has to offer.

Routes and Distances

From either north or south, take U.S. 101 to Ventura and turn inland on California 33. Follow 33 into the hills for fourteen miles to the edge of the little town of Ojai. Start looking for the Ojai Valley Inn sign to the right, just across from a large stable and horse ranch. Turn right at the sign, and then immediately right again into the inn's well-marked entrance road.

Accommodations

As you drive up, you will see what appears to be a single-story building, Spanish-style with a red tile roof. It is set on a broad, tree-shaded lawn and surrounded by a golf course. Around behind, however, where the hill on which the original buildings were built falls off, the inn appears massive, a full five stories tall, and it is obvious that additional rows of guest quarters were added at different times over the years.

Since the rooms have been staggered down the hillside, they all have a splendid view across the golf course and down the length of a scenic arm of the Ojai Valley and get the sun all day long on their decks and terraces.

The inn has 110 rooms, of some six different configurations. The smallest and least expensive are in one of the older, outlying cottages, while the more expensive rooms are in the upper portion of the new additions. Room prices here are determined primarily by their size, with some of the higher priced rooms very spacious and luxurious indeed. At the middle of the price range are rooms in the original inn building which, instead of having decks and terraces, open onto small, semiprivate lawns on the view side.

A typical unit in one of the newer additions is furnished with two twin beds side by side under a single headboard, two big comfortable

All rooms overlook the Ojai Valley

lounge chairs with individual side tables and reading lamps, two smaller upholstered lounge chairs, a card table, color television, and a telephone. Opening off this room is a small dressing room with a closet and vanity, and the bath. A connecting door to the next unit makes it possible to combine the two into a two-room, two-bath suite.

Among the amenities you will enjoy are a bowl of fresh fruit on the table when you arrive and maid service that includes turning down the beds at night and providing fresh towels if the regular supply has been exhausted during the day.

Automobile parking is generally close to most units, although there are a few where you will want help with your luggage.

Activities

The oak-studded Ojai golf course has two different and distinct nines, with the second definitely the longer and harder. Both nines are over beautiful, rolling terrain and are carefully maintained. Ojai is a player's course, used primarily by inn guests and a limited country club membership, with no effort made to attract big tournaments or publicity, so that the course remains relatively uncrowded and enjoyable to play. Even though it is a favorite of Southern California's experienced players, it remains remarkably inexpensive, with greens fees of only $12 during midweek and $15 on weekends.

After golf, the most popular pastime at Ojai is probably eating and sipping drinks on the broad, colorful terrace under the oak trees, watching golfers come and go. But that properly belongs in the dining section of this book, so the tennis center, a relatively recent addition to the inn property, should come next on the activities list. There are eight new, individually fenced, championship-quality courts at the center, along with a pro shop, ball machines, and a qualified teaching professional. Four of the courts are lighted for night play. Fees for guests for court use are $7 per person per day, except on the midweek package plans under which court use (and greens' fees for golfers) are included in the basic charge.

The original Ojai Inn had a strong western flavor that emphasized horseback riding as a primary recreational activity. That is by no means lost in the modern operation, and the inn still maintains a stable of twenty-five saddle horses, managed by "Doc" Pearce, chief wrangler for many years. Rides can be scheduled at any time for groups of any size, and are an especially popular activity with young people during the summer months, while their elders play golf and tennis.

Playground equipment scattered on the property helps to keep other youngsters diverted, as does the heated pool located behind a sheltering row of eucalyptus in front of the main lodge.

A well-kept croquet course on the lawn next to the lodge provides yet another diversion, and there is an eighteen-hole putting green next to the first tee of the golf course and a practice driving range close to the pro shop.

The first golf tee is immediately adjacent to the inn itself, but the tennis center is a short drive or ten-minute walk back down the entrance road. The stables are on the far side of the golf course, outside of walking range, but the wrangler will send a car for anyone lacking transportation.

Dining

Meals at the Ojai Valley Inn are a compelling testimonial to the benefits of the American Plan, under which meals are included in room prices. It works particularly well at inns—like this one—where guests will take most of their meals on the premises. Under the American Plan, the number of meals and the basic menu are relatively predictable, so the chef and kitchen staff can plan and prepare efficiently.

Breakfast is served every morning in the aptly named Vista Room, overlooking the golf course and the blue hills of the Sierra Madres beyond. It is buffet style, with a bountiful selection of fruit, eggs, meat, potatoes, and rolls. Golfers anxious to get out on the course can move through the line quickly, while those with less pressing plans can take the meal in as leisurely a manner as they like.

The Ojai's garden terrace is sheltered by giant oaks

Good as the breakfasts are, Ojai's most famous meals are the buffet luncheons on the terrace. These were what we had heard most about before our visit, and we were not disappointed. The buffet itself, including hot and cold foods, is set up in the Topa Topa Room just off the terrace. You help yourself, then move outside to one of the white wrought-iron tables shaded by gaily colored umbrellas. The terrace looks out through the limbs of gnarled giant oaks to activity on the golf course directly alongside. The food is superb, and again conducive to lingering and enjoying.

After lunch, it is a good idea to play some tennis, take a long walk, or otherwise prepare yourself for the evening meal. Dinner is served in the combined Vista and Garden rooms, and is a much more formal affair. Men are required to wear jackets, and ties are "requested"; women wear dresses or dressy pant suits.

In the evening, each table has a fresh floral centerpiece arranged around a single lighted candle. The soft lighting reflected on mellow wood walls and paneled vaulted ceilings establishes a perfect backdrop for the elegant continental dinner. It starts with a relish tray, hot or cold soup, and a salad. The entrées include such seafood items as swordfish, scampi, and abalone, along with a variety of meat and fowl dishes. Marvelous pastries and sundaes follow, with the coffee, to complete the meal. An added treat is dinner dancing on Friday and Saturday nights, and in the summer months, both dinner and dancing are moved out onto the terrace, under the stars.

Pierpont Inn

Distances:
From downtown Los Angeles—65 miles; allow 1¼ hours
From San Francisco—366 miles; allow 7 to 8 hours

Features:
Well-known, long-established inn, prominently located right on Highway 101; proximity to Los Angeles makes it particularly convenient for quick getaways and stopovers; ocean views, easy beach access, good food, and reasonable prices

Activities:
Swimming in heated pool or ocean, tennis, racquetball, access to the Channel Islands

Seasons:
Year-round

Rates:
$46 to $52 for two people: suites $75 and up

Address:
550 Sanjon Road, Ventura, California 93001

Phone:
(805) 643-6144

The Pierpont Inn, just 65 miles from Los Angeles

Pierpont Inn has been owned and managed by the same family for three generations, and has been a prominent part of this community for as long as anybody in these parts can remember. As such it has always been—and still is—an activities center and gathering place for local people during the day, while at night it fills up with people from Santa Barbara and Thousand Oaks and Ojai who come over perhaps for a little time on the beach, as well as for dinner. The result is that the inn's big dining room is full all day long and constantly abuzz with activity.

At one time the inn was beach-front property, set on a low bluff just behind the sand, and operated as a beach resort. In time, however, the freeway was built, placing a concrete barrier between the inn and the sea, and changing its character irrevocably. There is still easy access to the beach, under an overpass, but the inn has settled into a new existence as a getaway place for short, quick trips, or as a stopover point for people traveling the coast, rather than as a destination resort for long vacations.

As a stopover, Pierpont Inn is hard to beat. There aren't many places you can stay when traveling where you can swim in the ocean, play tennis, and have fabulous food all for the price of a modest motel room. Those who have discovered the inn are quick to take advantage of this: they allow an extra day for a business trip, take their spouses along, and stop at the Pierpont Inn to combine work with a little fun.

Or, for the spur-of-the-moment two- or three-day getaway, the inn has enough rooms that reservations are often available on short notice, and it is an easy drive from a dozen cities.

You will quickly be distracted from the constant hum of traffic by the fresh ocean breezes, sweeping views toward the Channel Islands, pleasant gardens shaded by picturesque cypresses, and one of California's best tennis and swim clubs, available for guests' use, no farther than the other side of the parking lot.

Routes and Distances

From the south, on U.S. 101, after passing through Ventura look for the Sanjon Road–Vista del Mar Drive exit. Take it, and almost immediately you will come upon the steep Pierpont Inn entrance drive.

Coming from the north, go past the inn, which is plainly visible on the left, and take the next exit, Seaward Avenue. At the end of the ramp is a traffic light. Turn right at the light onto Harbor Boulevard. About a minute later you will come to the Sanjon Road. Take another right there, go under an overpass, and you will be at the inn's entrance drive.

Accommodations

Way back in 1928 an exclusive men's club in the Pierpont district of Ventura was remodeled to make the Pierpont Inn. That original building, now containing the restaurant, offices, and various meeting rooms and shops, is still the core of the operation, while two big wings have been added, one on either side, to provide the rooming accommodations.

The room rate schedule is simple here because there are no seasonal variations and only two basic tariffs, one for the newer west wing addition, and one for the older east wing.

The east wing rooms, which are all similar in size, represent the most economical choice on the schedule. Being the oldest, they were built when the hotel rooms were just meant for sleeping, and therefore are relatively small. They have, however, recently been completely renovated and redecorated by a designer who creatively used every bit of available space without making it appear too utilitarian.

Each room is furnished with either a double bed or twin beds, along with a small table, side chairs, and a television set. They all have small dressing areas and bathrooms that have been updated with new fixtures. The big advantage of east wing rooms, in addition to their price, is their location around a lovely pool and patio area, onto which the ground floor rooms open directly.

The more expensive west wing was added more recently, so the

Accommodations in the old wing

rooms are bigger and are equipped with more modern fixtures and furniture. It also has a few two-room suites, but with that exception, all the rooms in this wing are identical in size and price and vary only in that some have two double beds and some just one. All have room for card tables and chairs, as well as an easy chair to relax in. Other attributes include a nice dressing area, modern baths with walk-in showers, and either furnished balconies or, on the ground level, patios. Many of these west wing rooms have ocean views, which you might think to ask for when making reservations.

The two-room suites are only twenty-one dollars more than a double room in this wing, making a good arrangement for family use. They have large living rooms with studio couches that convert to twin beds at night, while the bedrooms have two double beds. Both rooms share one large bath which has a tub and shower and, for a touch of elegance, a bidet.

Activities

The Pierpont Racquet Club is a private club, separate from the inn but on the same property. It leases its premises from the inn, and there is an arrangement between them that allows inn guests to enjoy most club membership privileges for only a modest fee.

The club has a fine, big clubhouse that contains a full pro shop,

A championship court at Pierpont Tennis Club

snack bar, several viewing areas, twelve tennis courts with lights, six racquetball courts, a big indoor swimming pool, and a Jacuzzi and saunas. The tennis courts are all of championship quality, with wide sidelines, individual fencing and screening, and colorful plantings along the connecting walkways. This is a very active, top-notch club, and if you enjoy racket sports, do not fail to bring your equipment when you come to the Pierpont Inn.

In the opposite direction, and nearly as close, a one-minute walk under the highway overpass will take you to the Buenaventura State Beach and Park. The beach here is about a mile long, with a public fishing pier at one end and the big, grassy park at the other. It has a shallow gradient, good for swimming, and is well guarded and safe. Surf casting for perch is popular in the early morning. There is a good path for bicycling and jogging along the outer perimeter, but the beach itself is ideal for walking or jogging on the firm sand at the water's edge.

From the inn, it is easy to see the oil platforms blinking like lighted Christmas trees at night, and in the daytime, beyond the platforms, the outline of the nation's fortieth and newest national park, the Channel Islands, is plain to see. The Channel Islands Park headquarters is two miles from the inn, and worth a visit if time allows. Drive out of the inn, under the overpass onto Harbor Boulevard, and go left to Spinnaker Drive at the fourth traffic light. Take a right on Spinnaker Drive, and follow it all the way around to the head of the harbor. You will make a half-circle around the Ventura Marina, where you will see what is likely to be the thickest forest of sailboat masts you have even seen. The brand-new park headquarters building is at the extreme end of the drive. There, you will find ample graphic display material, plus a twenty-minute film, shown continuously, that thoroughly describes the islands and the reasons for their preservation. Should you determine to explore the subject further, the park people will explain how to make a reservation for one of the day-long launch excursions that circumnavigate the various islands, with occasional conducted tours ashore to see the wildlife. If you are lucky, from November through April you might also see some migrating whales as you go.

Dining

Dining here seems to be the number one attraction, both for lunch and dinner, judging by the jammed condition of the parking lot at both those times of day. Even at breakfast there are always a lot of people coming and going, although at that time only one of the four dining areas is open.

As with the rooms, one of the reasons for the restaurant's popularity is its reasonable prices. The other is illustrated by the answer a waitress gave us when we asked why the place seemed to be so busy. She paused a moment, then responded matter-of-factly, "Because it's the best restaurant in Ventura." A good enough reason, and one we don't question.

It is especially pleasant at lunchtime to have your meal in the bar from where, on a clear day, you have a good view of the Channel Islands. The lunch menu offers a variety of appealing and bountifully heaped salads, excellent hot and cold sandwiches, and a daily special which often includes a spicy, hot Mexican dish.

The dinner menu is huge, with at least thirty entrées to choose from, plus more daily specials. All available areas are in use then, and usually at full capacity. An added attraction is entertainment six nights a week in the big, roomy bar. Monday through Wednesday an individual entertainer is featured, and on Thursday through Saturday evenings a group provides music for dancing.

Not too far from the inn is another place to eat, especially for seafood fans. You can drive to the Pier Fishhouse, or even stroll north along the beach for about fifteen minutes to the long fishing pier on which it is located. If you're not interested in a sit-down meal, particularly for lunch, there is also a snack bar farther out toward the pier's end.

Central Desert
Getaways

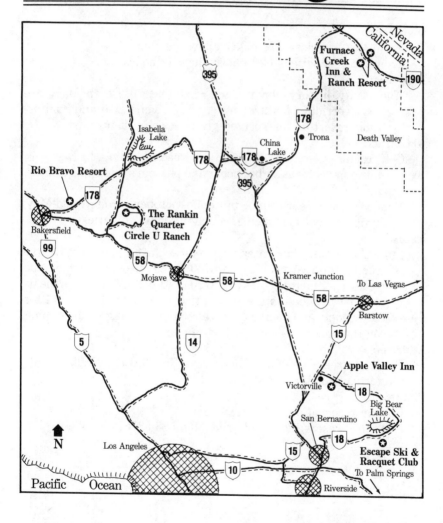

Furnace
Creek
Inn &
Ranch Resort

Nevada
California

190

395

178

Isabella
Lake

China
Lake

Trona

Death Valley

Rio Bravo Resort

178

178

178

395

Bakersfield

99

The Rankin
Quarter
Circle U Ranch

58

Mojave

58

Kramer Junction

To Las Vegas

58

Barstow

15

5

14

Apple Valley Inn

Victorville

18

Big Bear
Lake

San Bernardino

18

N

Los Angeles

15

Escape Ski &
Racquet Club

Pacific   Ocean

10

To Palm Springs

Riverside

Furnace Creek Inn & Ranch Resort

Distances:
From Los Angeles—278 miles; allow 5½ hours
From San Francisco—539 miles; allow 11 hours

Features:
The beauty, history, climate, and remoteness of Death Valley are the overriding features here, with a venerable and comfortable resort an unexpected green oasis in their midst

Activities:
Golf, tennis, swimming, bicycling, horseback riding, browsing in museum; copious sight-seeing and photographic opportunities

Seasons:
Ranch is open year-round; inn open October through mid-May; summer heat is extreme, curtailing most activities

Rates:
Inn is American Plan: rates include breakfast and dinner; deluxe rooms for two people are $140 to $145, depending on the season; standard rooms are $120 to $140. At the ranch, meals are not included in the room price; cabins are $42 to $44 for two people and deluxe rooms are $44 to $61, again depending on the season

Address:
Furnace Creek Inn or Furnace Creek Ranch, Death Valley, California 92328

Phone:
For inn reservations: (619) 786-2345
For ranch reservations: toll free (800) 528-6376

Furnace Creek Inn below the Sombre Funeral Mountains

From the lowest point of the valley floor, 282 feet below sea level, to the forbidding snowcapped tops of the bordering mountains, Death Valley encompasses a vertical drop of over two miles, almost twice the much-heralded depth of Grand Canyon. Moreover, it averages a bare 1½ inches of rainfall each year, and consistently records the hottest summer temperatures in all North America. It is, in short, a place of extremes: extreme climatological changes, extreme and convoluted landscapes, extreme isolation, and above all, extremes of ever-changing color and beauty.

Once you enter the valley, you will see few signs of life. No rabbits or chipmunks scuttle across the road, no bugs fly, not even a bird wheels anywhere in the sky. The trip into the valley is a memorable experience in its own right. You cross a wide, high desert, populated by Joshua trees, and then a series of ever higher mountain ranges separated by deep valleys, each revealing a stark new landscape with its own strange plants and cacti, and wide vistas in every direction where distances are deceptive due to the clean, dry air. If you have read about the early explorers and adventurers who tried to cross these sere ranges on foot and horseback in California's early days, you will be overwhelmed with wonder at how they did it, and with sympathy for the suffering that must have accompanied every trip.

It is all the more surprising, then, to arrive at the Furnace Creek Resort and discover that there is an oasis in the middle of this vast

A twenty-mule-team wagon train at the Harmony Borax Works

wasteland. Thanks to water channeled from springs high in the Funeral Mountains, this site is a green haven full of long windbreaks of tamarisk trees and groves of stately date palms, and a lush eighteen-hole golf course, and swimming pools and tennis courts.

White saline minerals, principally borax, still much in evidence on the valley floor, drew the early pioneers. At one time the U.S. Borax Company conducted extensive mining operations here, with Furnace Creek as its natural headquarters. A ranch was maintained as a way station for the men and mules of the borax trade, and on a high knoll overlooking the valley an elegant lodge was constructed to house visiting executives and dignitaries. In time, new deposits of borax were discovered in less forbidding climates and the borax business went into decline in Death Valley, but the Borax Company foresaw possibilities of attracting tourists, and in 1926 converted the lodge into an inn. Additional rooms and facilities were built for that purpose, constructed principally of native fieldstone and adobe, with much of the work done by local Indians of the Panamint tribe. The result was a beautiful and superbly comfortable structure for its time and location, and it soon achieved wide renown. Regular service in and out was conducted by Ford trimotor aircraft and open-top touring cars.

In time the ranch, about a half-mile from the inn, was also converted to tourist facilities with the construction of cottages and a restaurant. In 1933 President Hoover signed a bill making all of Death Valley a National Monument; all, that is, except the Furnace Creek enclave still owned by the Borax Company. Creation of the park effectively eliminated the possibility of any other developments, however, so that the ranch and the inn, and a small facility at Stovepipe Wells ten miles distant, remain the only possible places to stay in the whole valley.

The Borax Company, tiring of the hostelry business, ultimately closed the last of its mines and sold off its properties in the area. The Fred Harvey Company thereupon acquired the management rights, and today operates both the inn and the ranch, maintaining them as separate entities, although with many mutually supporting and interchangeable features. The inn is still the fancier and more expensive address of the two, with its own separate tennis courts and pool, better views, and dining limited to guests. The ranch, situated next to the golf course, is quite informal compared to the inn. It has its own pool, tennis courts, and restaurants, with some cabins and a quantity of motellike rooming accommodations. There are also a general store, a service station, a post office, and a small museum on the premises.

Clustered nearby are an airstrip, two parks for recreational vehicles, a campground, and another larger museum, all maintained by the Park Service. These, of course, attract many people who add to the crowds in the store and restaurants, and assure that the ranch is always alive with activity.

Routes and Distances

From Los Angeles, probably the fastest route to Death Valley is to go east on Interstate 10 to the intersection with Interstate 15 near Fontana. Then go north on 15 for thirty miles to the junction where U.S. 395 begins, just below Victorville. Take 395 north for seventy miles, but halfway up, at Kramer Junction, top off your gas tank (especially if you use diesel) and see to any other automotive necessities. There are gas stations at Trona and at Furnace Creek itself, but they are apt to have only the basics, so be forewarned. North of Kramer Junction, at Johannesburg, switch off 395 to California 178, the well-marked route to Trona. After Johannesburg you start the series of mountain ascents and passes crossing the El Paso, Slate, and Panamint ranges. You might see some wild burros here, descendants of animals turned loose by early prospectors; but after Emigrant Pass there will be no more wildlife. Just beyond Emigrant Pass, 178 joins with California 190, which loops down through Stovepipe Wells directly to Furnace Creek.

Coming from the San Francisco Bay area, drive to Bakersfield and then take California 58 to Mojave. At Mojave, go north on California 14 to intersect with 178 at the Inyokern cutoff. Take 178 through China Lake to Trona, then proceed as above to 190 and Furnace Creek.

For pilots, Furnace Creek has a good 2900-foot landing strip, lighted at night and with fuel available. Pick-up service from either the ranch or the inn will be furnished on a few minutes' notice.

Accommodations

By road, the inn and the ranch are about a half-mile apart. The big, sprawling inn is backed up to the mountains on a promontory at the mouth of Furnace Creek, and the ranch is down on the flats below, with both kept fresh and green by piped water from the mountains.

It was in 1926—the same year that another grand old hotel listed in this book, La Quinta in the Coachella Valley, was built—that Indian labor put the finishing touches on the inn, and it was opened for business. The intriguing thing is that from its very inception, despite the remote and exotic location, Furnace Creek Inn was known for quality service, and established a solid reputation for charm and hospitality that has not since diminished.

Today, it provides two basic accommodations, deluxe and standard rooms. The deluxe rooms are relatively large, with fine outlooks over the garden and desert. Each is furnished with a king bed or two

Date palms shield guests from the Death Valley heat

twins and has a comfortable sitting area with two chairs and a table. The newest deluxe units in the north wing have the additional attraction of private balconies.

Standard rooms are similar but slightly smaller; the main difference is that they are located on the opposite side of the building, where views are restricted.

Having been built so long ago, none of the rooms have the modern nicety of dressing rooms, but they do have good-size baths and all are air-conditioned and equipped with telephones. For television you must go down to watch the communal sets in the big Victorian lobby or in the cocktail lounge.

In some ways, the construction and design of the inn building is reminiscent of medieval castles. This is due in part to the immense amount of stone masonry used in construction and in part to the many levels of terraces and galleries and the way they are connected by tunnels and winding stone staircases. A cool blue swimming pool is incorporated into the design at the base of the lower level, and beside the pool is a large, luxuriant oasis of date palms on a steep hillside laced with little paths and watered by a clear stream tumbling down its center.

At the ranch, where a strongly western flavor and casual atmosphere prevail, the accommodations and general layout are different from those at the inn. There is no attempt at elegance here, but the quarters are comfortable and the prices reasonable. The oldest units consist of twenty-five cabins, which the management says are always the first ones to fill up, probably because they are the least expensive, and because pets are allowed in the cabins but not in any other units. The cabin rooms are small and simply furnished, with two double beds, a chair and a dresser, and a bath with shower. They are air-conditioned, of course, but have no telephones or television sets.

The other quarters at the ranch are newer. These are deluxe rooms located in a group of one-story and two-story buildings facing the pool, tennis courts, and golf fairways. Best described as good motel rooms, they are comfortably furnished with two double beds and standard motel furniture. They have small dressing alcoves, or patios, and telephones, but no television sets. There are 225 rooms here, as compared with 69 at the inn.

Activities

The first order of business—or pleasure—for visitors to Death Valley is seeing the valley itself. The variety of vantage points and ever-changing lighting and colors at every scene make sight-seeing an endless series of delights. Much of this is necessarily done by automobile, but there are close-in expeditions that can be taken on foot or, better yet, on horseback or by bicycle. Bikes can be rented at

Playing golf in a desert oasis

the gasoline station, and a nice ride is to set out uphill on California 190 for about three miles to Zabriskie Point, where an outlook of fabulous proportions awaits. It is a bit of a stiff pull up the hill, but well worth it, and the time spent seeing the sights affords a chance to rest. Then, there is an exhilarating downhill trip, all the way back past the inn and the ranch, and then along a bike path that parallels the road for another mile, terminating at the old Harmony Borax Works. Here you can dismount and explore a place steeped in history—the starting point for the famous twenty-mule teams that once hauled borax processed at the works 165 miles overland to the railroad at Mojave. The story of Harmony is fascinating, and by roaming the ruins and reading the placards, and later supplementing this with a visit to the Death Valley Museum, you will piece it all together and have an excellent understanding of the legendary life and times of that historic era of a hundred years ago. The museum is operated by the Park Service, and is next to the ranch. Park Service representatives will provide you with written itineraries for exploration trips all through Death Valley. Among the most interesting are the 120-mile round trip to Aguereberry Point, the all-day trip north to Scotty's Castle, and the half-day trip to Dante's View and Badwater.

Behind the ranch, on the edge of the desert, are the stables from which regular guided rides are conducted twice a day, and special rides by appointment. The trails fan out onto the salt flats where Chinese laborers once gathered the borax "cottonball" to be refined at the Harmony works. Going out by horseback is probably the most memorable way you can experience Death Valley and appreciate what it must have been like in its heyday when animal transportation was the only thing available, even to the most affluent.

Between sight-seeing excursions you can fit in golf or tennis and swim or bake around the pools. The golf course is as pretty as can be, studded with palms and always brillant green, but flat all the way and not difficult. Par is seventy for men and seventy-two for women, with moderate greens fees of $12 for eighteen holes. Carts are available, but not required.

Tennis is best at the inn, where four very good, lighted courts are free to inn guests. The ranch has only two courts, but they are also available without charge to people staying at the ranch. For lessons, a pro is available at the inn courts for both inn and ranch guests.

An unusual experience is to take a walk through the 32-acre date orchard that lies next to the ranch and golf course. Palm trees are said to thrive best when they have their feet in water and their heads in the sun, and these trees have both to the nth degree. The trees are heavy producers, and you can pick a few dates off the ground to sample as you walk about, or buy some in quantity to take home.

In the dry air, nothing rots or rusts very fast, and old wagons, engines, and other machinery from a hundred years ago are still lying about outdoors in a remarkable state of preservation. A large sampling of these historic items is housed in a compound just across from the ranch restaurants and next to the little borax museum. The items offer a chance to study some of the industrial antiquities and lifestyles of one of America's great growth periods, and there is no charge to visitors.

Dining

There are five different restaurants within the complex, offering a range of selections and prices. The nearest town for groceries and supplies, we found out from one of our waitresses who makes the trip weekly, is Las Vegas, 140 miles away—a bit of incidental information that helps underscore the remoteness of the setting, and the difficult logistics involved in keeping the resort supplied with everything these five restaurants need. That it is accomplished, and with the overall high quality of food served, is a credit to the organization.

Two of the restaurants are at the inn and three at the ranch. The inn operates on an American Plan, which includes breakfast and dinner in the basic room rates, so its main dining room is open only to inn guests. It is a fairly formal room—in the evening men wear jackets

The general store and cafeteria at the ranch

and women wear dresses or pant suits, and the complete menu always includes appetizers, soup and salad, beef or seafood entrées, desserts, and beverages.

The Oasis Supper Club, a somewhat cozier dining room downstairs, is less formal and is not restricted to inn guests. Next to this are the bar and lounge. Both rooms are notable for their walls of the same natural fieldstone that forms the building's massive foundations. The Oasis Room has a dance floor in the center, with tables arranged around the perimeter, and dance music plays nightly. The menu is short, but offers some very good seafood items, especially the prawns in a special caper sauce, the steaks, and other beef entrées such as bourguignon fondue for two, or the grenadine of thin-sliced tenderloin cooked with great flourish right at tableside. (Because of their American Plan arrangement, inn guests who elect to eat in The Oasis Room instead of the dining room get a flat $15 credit against their dinner check.)

Inn guests are on their own for lunch. The dining room is open, if they want to eat there, and on nice days it extends service to poolside, or guests can go to the ranch or pick up sandwiches at the cafeteria for a picnic in the desert.

All of the ranch restaurants are casual and informal. The Coffee Shop is open all day, from 7:00 A.M. to 9:30 P.M. The Cafeteria next

door is a good place for early birds, since breakfast is served beginning at 5:30 A.M. It closes at 9:00 A.M., then opens again from 11:00
A.M. to 1:00 P.M. for lunch and from 5:00 P.M. to 8:30 P.M. for dinner.

The other alternative at the ranch is the Steak House, open only
for dinner. The setting is intriguing, with candles at each table providing the only light. Steak, salad, and red wine are the favorites
here, and the meals are well prepared and reasonably priced. Service
is on a first-come, first-served basis, but if you have to wait you can do
so next door in the colorful Corkscrew Saloon, where they will call you
when your table is ready.

Rio Bravo Resort

Distances:

From downtown Los Angeles—114 miles; allow 2½ hours

From San Francisco—306 miles; allow 6 hours

From Bakersfield—12 miles; allow 15 minutes

Features:

A lushly landscaped, relatively new, fully equipped resort that features tennis as its premier activity, but offers a wide variety of other diversions, in addition to excellent dining and comfortable accommodations

Activities:

Tennis, golf, river rafting and inner-tubing, horseback riding, swimming, and sunbathing

Seasons:

Year-round

Rates:

$85 for two people in most rooms, a few one- and two-bedroom suites at higher prices

Address:

11200 Lake Ming Road, Star Route 4, Box 501, Bakersfield, California 93306

Phone:

(805) 872-5000

The Rio Bravo Lodge

Who would guess, with all of the fine tennis facilities up and down the California coast and throughout the sunny desert resorts, that "one of the ten finest facilities in the nation" would be found tucked in the brown hills of Kern County, just east of Bakersfield. But that is the accolade *Tennis Magazine* has bestowed on Rio Bravo Resort, a nineteen-court complex built seven years ago in the heart of the Rio Bravo Ranch, a 10,000-acre stretch of land owned and operated by the George Nickel family.

The resort is no more than a speck on the overall property, which boasts a long and illustrious history. Dating as far back as 1776, when American revolutionaries were struggling in the East to found the United States, Spanish priests were exploring for the first time the land on which Rio Bravo lies. The property begins at the point where the roiling Kern River pours through a steep canyon coming down from the Sierra Nevadas and some of its water, diverted for irrigation, maintains the ranch land as an island of green among the surrounding brown foothills.

Rio Bravo is an operating ranch with many hundreds of acres of citrus groves and hay and pasture lands, plus thousands of acres of surrounding open range. In the middle of all this is tiny Ming Lake, the resort and tennis club, an airstrip, a golf course, and the beginnings of an ambitious residential community.

Until fairly recently, the resort was known as the Rio Bravo Tennis Ranch because its outstanding tennis facility was the main attraction, but since then other activities, including golf, horseback riding, and river rafting, have been added and the name changed simply to Rio Bravo Resort to reflect the diversification. The resort is operated on a year-round basis and the weather here at the foot of the San Joachin Valley is generally ideal for all outdoor sports, marred only by occasional winter fog and a few uncomfortably hot days in midsummer.

Routes and Distances

From either north or south, take the California 99 freeway to Bakersfield and turn east on the well-marked California 178 freeway. Rio Bravo is approximately twelve miles from Bakersfield. Continue on 178 until you pass Comanche Drive on the right. Immediately after that, look for a left turn onto Alfred Harrell Highway. (A large Rio Bravo sign helps identify this turn.) Make the turn and follow it a short distance until you reach a well-marked directory to Rio Bravo's lodge.

Accommodations

Like everything else at Rio Bravo, the accommodations reflect the tasteful planning that went into the master scheme for the resort. Guests are put up in four handsome lodges clustered in an oasis of green lawn, colorful flowers, and graceful trees, a setting that contrasts markedly with the stark landscape surrounding it. All four of the lodges are within easy range of the tennis courts, pools, and Jacuzzi, and just a short stroll from the dining room and lounge.

These two-story buildings have facades of roughcut wood siding and modified mansard roofs, which give them a distinctive appearance. Balconies open off all of the upper-level rooms, creating shade for the patios on the level below. This is a bonus on hot summer days, even though all of the rooms are air-conditioned for year-round comfort.

The most attractive characteristic of the accommodations is their overall spaciousness, from the wide, airy hallways and staircases to the large square rooms. All of the 112 units are the same size and have comfortable sitting areas more than ample for entertaining guests. Most of the rooms are furnished with a king bed or twin beds, plus two overstuffed chairs with a lamp table between in one corner—a most comfortable arrangement for reading or watching television. The other corner, furnished with a game table and chairs, illuminated by a hanging lamp, makes a cozy spot for playing cards or writing letters.

The only other units at Rio Bravo are the studios. These rooms, which have wood-burning fireplaces and wet bars, are furnished with couches that convert to beds. Each of the studios is connected to the room on either side, and can be opened up to make a one- or two-

Tennis, with the Sierra Nevadas in the distance

bedroom suite. A request for this type of accommodation is usually done with entertaining in mind.

Activities

Tennis is still undisputed as the number one interest at Rio Bravo but, with the advent of the recently completed private golf course and the ever-increasing popularity of river rafting and inner-tubing on the Kern River, activities at the resort have definitely expanded, and offer something for just about every taste.

To those familiar with the Rio Bravo tennis complex, it will come as no surprise that *Tennis Magazine* rates it so highly. The major part of the facility belongs to a private tennis club, but seven courts are set aside for the exclusive use, free of charge, of guests of the resort. A fully equipped pro shop and the services of two full-time professionals are at the disposal of Rio Bravo guests, as well as private club members, and every effort is made to line up games for those who are interested.

Most of the courts have excellent lighting systems, since soaring temperatures in the summer make morning and evening the most popular times to play. Midday is a good time to laze around the pool and enjoy reading, or perhaps a bridge game, in the shade of one of the several poolside gazebos.

Guests raft the nearby Kern River

Although it has recently taken on a dramatic new dimension, golf is not new at Rio Bravo. The public Kern River golf course, which is just a short distance from the resort, has provided an adequate facility for golfers since the resort opened, but now a brand-new championship course at Rio Bravo itself is generating a great deal of enthusiasm among discriminating players. This is a private club, whose membership comes mostly from Bakersfield and which has its own pro shop, clubhouse, and snack bar. It is conveniently close to the resort, whose guests are extended full privileges but, of course, are expected to pay a greens fee.

River rafting and inner-tubing on the Kern River are becoming more popular with Rio Bravo guests each year. Staff members at the resort transport river rafters and inner-tubers to a section of the river where a two-mile course begins, and a couple of hours later they are waiting at the finish point to retrieve the water-soaked adventurers. Plenty of white-water stretches make it exciting, but all trips are supervised and guided. The fee for the outing includes all equipment, but there must be a minimum of eight in the group for rafting and five for inner-tubing.

Another focal point of interest in the spring and on lazy summer days is the Equestrian Center, just a short distance away. Guests can sign up for guided horseback rides on trails along the river and through the surrounding hills. Sometimes, on warm summer evenings, groups are gathered for hayrides and outdoor barbecues.

Dining

The dining facility serves the dual purpose of handling both members of the private club and guests of the resort. Located in the tennis clubhouse building, the dining room can seat about eighty people in an informal but elegant area that has a high, open-beamed ceiling dominated by a huge chandelier and walls paneled with a mellow, dark-toned wood. A big stone fireplace in one corner of the room provides a comforting glow whenever chilly evening air comes down off the Sierras. Directly adjacent to the dining room are a spacious player's lounge and bar sharing a view directly overlooking the tennis courts, which usually provide an action backdrop for both luncheon and dinner guests.

The dining room serves all three meals, seven days a week, and the staff takes a high measure of pride in the successful operation of the establishment. Tables are elegantly set for the dinner hour, and soft candlelight at each setting reveals such niceties as a bouquet of fresh flowers encircled by thin-stemmed, bell-shaped wineglasses, each filled with a starchy white napkin folded in the shape of a fan.

The menu is extensive, with not only a wide selection of beef and veal, as would be expected in cattle country, but also seafood and fowl dishes prepared by a chef who knows how to make his creations unusually attractive as well as tasty. Prices are reasonable, and in line with comparable restaurants.

Should a change of scene be desired, however, the drive back to Bakersfield is short enough (no more than fifteen minutes) to warrant a little exploration of the area's unique variety of Basque restaurants. These all serve their old country specialties "family style," meaning the food is brought to the table in bowls and platters from which all diners help themselves. The Château Basque at Union and First Street, the Chalet Basque at 200 Oak Street, and the Wool Growers at 620 East 19th Street are all good places to try this unusual cuisine.

The Rankin Quarter Circle U Ranch

Distances:

From Bakersfield—42 miles; allow 1 hour

From Los Angeles—143 miles; allow 3 hours

Features

A large working cattle ranch; also a lovely guest ranch in an isolated, superbly scenic location in the Tehachapi Mountains; family oriented during the summer months; everything is American Plan

Activities:

Trail riding, horsemanship, trout fishing, tennis, swimming in heated pool, hiking, lawn games, square dancing, hayrides, and barbecues

Seasons:

Mid-April through Thanksgiving. April 11 to May 27, June 2 to 11, and September 8 to November 23 are considered off-season; everything else is on season

Rates:

$69.50 per day or $465.50 per week for each person; children under twelve in room with parents, $52.50 and $345.50, respectively; off-season rates about $64.50 per day; rates are American Plan and include room, meals, horses, tennis and so on

Address:

Box 36, Caliente, California 93518

Phone:

Walker's Basin (805) 867-2511

With a guest list of forty, the ranch ensures a personal touch.

We were delighted, in our travels, to come across a place with our own last name, and even more pleased to find that we liked it very much. We hasten to add that the name is entirely coincidental, and that our only relationship to it is that of satisfied guests. There are a number of other fine resorts in Southern California where horseback riding and conducted trail rides are a part of the overall program, but for real horse lovers and for those who would like a sense of ranch life as it was in the early days of the West, there is no better choice than this Rankin Quarter Circle U Ranch.

Located deep in the Tehachapi Mountains of Kern County, the ranch is spread over 31,000 acres of high valley land in the remote Walker Basin. Five generations of Rankins have lived on the land and made their living here since the first arrived by covered wagon over 120 years ago and built the beautiful ranch house that is still the gracious center of activity.

The Quarter Circle U is one of the largest privately owned ranches in the entire West and is still primarily a working cattle ranch that presently runs about three thousand head of cattle. When the founder, Walker Rankin, first saw the land, he thought it would be particularly suitable for raising the white-faced Herefords he had seen in England, and he subsequently introduced the breed to this part of the country.

The ranch was well established and much as it is today when the

Civil War was raging in the South and the Pony Express was making trips through the valley. Later on, the drivers of Wells Fargo stage-coaches changed horses in an old barn still standing on the ranch, now used to store hay.

Many modern conveniences have been added since then: a lovely swimming pool, a tennis court, and a clubhouse, but they do not alter the fact that this is first and foremost a working operation. The guest facilities are less than twenty years old, but that has been ample time to attract a loyal clientele that loves the quiet, peaceful life, the ex-cellent ranch food, long daily rides, fishing in the little lake, or just plain sitting in the sun. Guests also enjoy the respite from a more hec-tic life, since there are no telephones, televisions, or radios.

The guest season on the ranch is about eight months of the year, usually beginning Easter week and running through Thanksgiving. Most guests come for at least a week, although some come for just a few days at a time. Everything is paid for in a single price on the American Plan, including the delightful meals, the horses, hayrides, picnics, and use of the tennis court and other facilities.

People come to the ranch from all over the country, but many Europeans, fascinated by the western way of life in America, have come to know it too. Much of the fun of being on the ranch stems from the gracious hospitality extended by the Rankins, who purposely limit their guest list to between thirty-six and forty so that guests can mingle easily and get to know one another.

The ranch is especially good for happy family vacations because a youth counselor takes care of children over four, keeping them pur-posefully engaged all day so that parents can pursue their own ac-tivities. The children love the country life and contact with animals, and you only hear them complain when it is time to leave. Most are so eager to stay that the Rankins have posted a sign on the bulletin board that pleads, "Please do not leave the ranch without your child."

About three-quarters of the guests here are repeaters, so new-comers should make reservations early, especially for the summer months when school is out. Reservations are often easier to get during the spring and fall, especially for spur-of-the-moment midweek getaways.

Routes and Distances

From Bakersfield, take California 58 east toward Mojave for twenty-five miles to the Caliente turnoff on the left. From the south, take California 14 north to Mojave and there go west on 58, across Tehachapi Summit, thirty-four miles to the Caliente road. From the turnoff, go north about two miles to Caliente (one post office, two houses, and a railway depot) and continue along the same road another three miles to a fork. Take the high road to the left, labeled

Guest cabins are widely spaced, shielded by trees

Cal Bodfish Road (not the one to the right, which goes to Lorraine and Twin Oaks). Continue for another thirteen miles of steep, winding, scenic mountain driving, and look for the Rankin Ranch's small sign on the right, just as you emerge onto the flat valley of Walker Basin. Much of the drive through the mountains is open range. Watch out for the Rankins' white-faced cattle, which you may encounter wandering along the road.

Accommodations

The guest quarters at the ranch are all nearly identical, so there are no hard choices to be made. Six cottages are scattered on the hillside behind the main ranch house, spaced for privacy and nestled in among groves of trees. There are two units in every cabin, each with a separate entrance, but dividing doors can be opened up to make one large suite.

The cabins are simple western-style structures, with pitched, open-beam ceilings and knotty-wood paneled walls. The floors are carpeted with patterned rugs and each room is furnished with two old-fashioned white iron beds, a double and a single, sporting bright red bedspreads. There is also a studio couch, so the rooms are just right for couples or for families with one or two small children. Other furniture includes a dresser, a couple of comfortable rattan chairs, and tables with good reading lamps. Each room has a big closet and a rather small bathroom with a tub. The accommodations are just about what you would want and expect on a ranch—rustic but comfortable—and are equipped with modern heating and air conditioning systems.

Activities

Walker Basin, between Breckenridge Mountain on one side and Piute Mountain on the other, is about as isolated, sparsely populated, and scenic as any place in the American West. If there is such a thing as typical ranch country, this is it, and the best way to see it and enjoy it is, naturally, on horseback. Just about everybody rides at the Quarter Circle U, where trail rides go out twice a day or more into the surrounding hills and mountainsides. Every year in the late fall, most of the ranch's three thousand head of cattle are driven by cowboys on horseback over a pass in the Breckenridge to a winter range on the other side. In the spring, when they are wild and sometimes rambunctious, they are driven back to the green pastures in Walker Basin and its surrounding hills, so on the trail rides you will encounter little bunches of skittish cattle here and there and can appreciate the job of the ranch hands who must hunt them down when they wander.

A seasoned wrangler leads every ride, assigning horses according to the rider's size and experience. A little preliminary instruction inside the corral is provided for beginners and children until they are ready to go out on the trail on the gentler mounts. The ranch is so vast that every ride will be different, showing you different landscape, birds, animals, and trees. Riders may spot quail, deer, doves, hawks, and—more rarely—black bear, and it is a good idea to carry a small tree guide so you can identify the many unusual species.

Youngsters from the city are often quick to become attached to the horses and like to hang around the corral and stables to watch the currying and saddling and occasionally carry a bucket of oats. They usually like to ride the same horse every day, and think of it as "their" horse, which occasions some sad partings when it's time to leave.

The counselor for younger children will keep them happy and active at riding and games and around the pool, and at dinnertime they have their own separate table.

The adults ride too, of course, or relax around the heated kidney-shaped pool. They also play tennis on the single hard-surface tennis court, which produces lively, high-bouncing balls due to the thin, dry air. Some of them like to hike, just for exercise, to hunt wildflowers, or see things they went by too fast on horseback, using the same trails as the riders. There are lawn games to play, too: shuffleboard, volleyball, and horseshoes.

A very special activity that everyone tries is fishing in Julia Lake, about three hundred yards from the ranch house. It is stocked with

Horse trails thread through the ranch's 31,000 acres

fighting rainbows, and everyone is allowed to catch one a day to be cooked in butter and garnished with fresh lemon slices for breakfast.

After dinner in the evening, activity concentrates in a building near the ranch house called The Lounge, which has a big, friendly, western-style living room filled with overstuffed chairs, sofas, and card tables. There is a large fireplace at one end where a fire blazes on cool evenings, a full-size pool table, and a small library. Sometimes movies are shown here at night, and occasionally there is old-fashioned western square dancing. On other nights there may be hayrides or outdoor barbecues, so there is hardly a time without something interesting going on.

To be properly equipped, guests should bring their own tennis gear, fishing tackle, riding boots, and swimming towels; the ranch can supply what is needed for all the other sports.

Dining

Big ranch breakfasts of hot cakes, eggs, bacon or sausage, fresh juice, and all that goes along with it are served every morning between 7:30 and 9:00 in the Garden Room, and guests straggle in as they please. Lunch is at 12:30 and dinner at 6:30, and everyone eats those meals together. Lunch is served outdoors on the terrace most of the time, and dinner is served inside in the light, cheery little Garden Room. The latter is actually an addition to the hundred-year-old ranch house, built as an adjunct to the original kitchen in order to take care of the guests. It contains just eight tables seating six people each in attractive white wicker chairs. The walls of this room are decorated with blown-up photos of old-time roundups and other ranch scenes from years gone by. You will always find fresh flowers on the tables, and every night a different setting of handmade tablecloths or placemats.

The custom in the evening is for the guests to gather for cocktails at 5:30 on the outdoor terrace in front of the Garden Room. Ice, mixers, and hors d'oeuvres will already be set out and waiting on the big glass-topped table, and guests can use their own liquor to mix what they like to drink, then spend a pleasant hour discussing the day's events and getting to know one another better. At 6:30 sharp a big bell mounted on a high pole rings to announce dinner in traditional ranch style.

Inside the dining room, a gracious young hostess makes table assignments as guests enter. Dinners are served family style, and careful preparation and excellent quality can be expected of everything from the soup and salad to dessert and coffee. Wine is not served by the ranch, but guests are welcome to bring their own and the waiter will be happy to provide wineglasses for those who do.

Apple Valley Inn

Distances:

From Los Angeles—90 miles; allow 1¾ hours

From San Diego—147 miles; allow 3 hours

Features:

A family-oriented inn offering diversions for children, good food, and generally reasonable prices; located in the "high desert," where it gets almost uninterrupted sunshine, but cool evenings

Activities:

Tennis and swimming, with golf and horseback riding nearby; nightly bar entertainment, Saturday night steak fries

Seasons:

Year-round, with busiest time Easter through Thanksgiving

Rates:

$55 for rooms for two people; suites and cottages $70 to $80; ask about special golf and three-day getaway packages

Address:

P.O. Box 5, Apple Valley, California 92307

Phone:

(619) 247-7271; toll free in California (800) 462-4084

At 3,200 feet, the Apple Valley Inn escapes the desert's swelter

Emphasis at the Apple Valley Inn changes with the season. In the summertime it is a low-key, informal, family-oriented resort, full of children playing and adults relaxing and having fun in the sun. In winter, however, after Thanksgiving, the pace quiets down, the children disappear, and the inn converts to a golf retreat and popular dinner spot, catering mainly to group meetings and business conferences.

In its summer resort phase, Apple Valley hasn't found it necessary to create any particular image. It has tennis, but isn't a tennis ranch. Its guests play golf at several good courses nearby, but it doesn't have its own golf course. It has a nice pool and plenty of sunshine, but it isn't a place where celebrities come to get tanned and be seen. In short, it is a hard place to categorize. But its relatively easy accessibility from greater Los Angeles, good summer weather, availability of reservations on short notice, generally reasonable prices, and friendly staff are advantages enough to assure its popularity.

Unlike the southerly desert around Palm Springs, where the heat brings most activities to a halt after Memorial Day, the high desert's season is just beginning to peak at that time, and has several more months still to run. The 3200-foot altitude here assures cooler, pleasant evenings which, combined with the very dry air, offer welcome relief to visitors coming from muggy conditions in the California valleys and coastal region.

The inn was originally built hard against a high, rocky hill in 1949, when land was cheap, which accounts for the way its many low, unassuming buildings are scattered on some twenty-eight acres. The main lodge, easily seen from the highway, houses the offices, restaurant and lounges, and a shop or two. The swimming pool lies in front of the lodge, with the tennis courts slightly to one side but quite close. The residences and gardens are dotted randomly about the grounds.

Routes and Distances

From Los Angeles, take any freeway east to Interstate 15 or 15E and go north on either one (they come together at Devore above San Bernardino) to Victorville. At Victorville, which is about thirty miles north of Devore, go east on California 18 for six miles to the town of Apple Valley. Apple Valley is a long, strung-out residential community with no precise center, but the inn is well marked and easy to see on the right side of the highway, just across from a contemporary church.

From San Diego, start on I-15, take the 15E cutoff then rejoin 15, as above, at Devore.

From Bakersfield and the west, take California 58 through Mojave to Barstow, then go south on I-15 to Victorville and east on California 18.

It may be startling to those traveling from the south how suddenly they emerge into the land of the strangely beautiful Joshua trees, once they reach the high desert following Cajon Pass in the San Gabriel Mountains. The Joshuas' abrupt appearance suggests how sensitive cacti and many other desert plants are to even slight changes of elevation and climate, as do the species variations along the way. Certain species disappear and are replaced by plants of radically different size and appearance over very short distances, offering living illustrations of adaptation to subtle changes in environment.

Accommodations

Among the first attractive features you will notice about Apple Valley are its pleasing landscaping and careful garden maintenance. Dramatic Joshua trees, palms, and tamarisks grow among the buildings, and there are banks of flowers and green lawns everywhere, with areas of pink, well-raked desert sand between.

The plantings and the dispersed layout of the accommodations afford a sense of privacy and casualness that help set Apple Valley apart. There are a few single cottages standing alone, several buildings containing two units, some with four, and others with six or eight. All are typical single-story California ranch-style buildings with red tile roofs and unpointed brick—simulating adobe—or western rough-sawn wood exteriors. A network of walkways connects the buildings, which all have parking areas nearby for ease of loading and unloading luggage.

Room layouts vary, but there are three fairly basic arrangements, which determine the tariffs. A typical room of the least expensive kind is simply furnished with twin beds, two lounge chairs, a writing

An old stage is the Apple Valley Inn's landmark

desk and chair, and a color television set. It will usually have a fairly large separate dressing room area with a closet, one or two vanities, and a small private bath.

For a few dollars more you can have a considerably larger room with a king bed and a gas fireplace—not a bad bargain.

At the upper end of the price range are the suites and cottages. A typical suite has two rooms that share a connecting bath, with a king bed in the bedroom and two daybeds in the sitting room, so that four persons can be accommodated. There is a gas fireplace in the sitting room, which is nice on the occasional cool evenings, along with a card table and four chairs and a small refrigerator.

The cottages are similarly equipped, but each is one large room, instead of two separate rooms, with a king bed on one side and a sitting area with a convertible sofa bed for extra people.

All the rooms have telephones, and most have a small entry area with one or two outside chairs for a place to sit in the evening.

When the inn was built thirty-three years ago, bathtubs were out of style and stall showers the mode. While this may not be as comfortable as you desire, the readiness of the inn's maintenance staff to provide you with convenience items and any other assistance required more than makes up for this.

Activities

The climate is pleasant year-round at Apple Valley, but the temperature variation from season to season alters activities considerably.

Golf is the unchallenged favorite sport here and is the only one played throughout the winter months as well as the rest of the year. The brisk, sunny days of winter, when the courses are a lush green, are an ideal time for golfers, and the inn caters to this crowd with special three-day package rates.

There are several good golf courses in the area, but most guests find it more convenient to play the closest one, just next door at the semiprivate Apple Valley Country Club. Reservations there can be made at the front desk of the inn. This is a challenging eighteen-hole course, and golfers are welcome to have lunch in its lovely clubhouse and to use its pro shop facilities. At present, the greens fee is a modest $10 on weekdays and $15 on weekends. Carts are required and rent for $14 a round for two players.

Two other nearby courses offer variety. The Hesperia Country Club, fifteen minutes southwest of the inn, has a good layout that is fun to play; the Spring Valley golf course is even closer. Reservations and tee-off times for these courses can also be arranged by the front desk.

The summer season and summer activities officially get under way early in April, in time for Easter weekend. The swimming pool

Joshua trees on the high desert

heat is turned on then, lounge furniture brought outside, and sun-bathers begin to appear on the terrace. The tennis courts, shuffle-board alleys, volleyball court, and a trim little nine-hole putting green all come into use, and are busy from then through November.

Old-timers will remember when the inn had its own stables next door and horseback riding was an important diversion. Unfortun-ately, arrangements with the concessionaire who owned the horses broke down, and it is now necessary for riders to drive about ten minutes into the desert to a very small stable called the Brown-Haven Ranch. Children will enjoy a visit to this unassuming place, since the people who run it are an eager young couple who keep an assortment of rabbits, pygmy goats, and other livestock to be seen and petted. Hour-long rides are conducted into the San Bernardino Mountains for very low rates—only $4 per hour in 1981.

The most popular weekly activity takes place on Saturday nights, when a big steak cookout is put on by the staff at the barbecue grounds up on the hillside above the inn. These are a regular event from Memorial Day until the end of the season in November.

Other evenings there is always some kind of entertainment at either the Western Bar Saloon or the Blossom Room. It might be a guitarist holding forth in the Western Bar on weekdays, and a group providing dance music on weekends in the Blossom Room, which has a rather spacious dance floor.

Tennis players should note that the four courts at Apple Valley do not purport to be of championship quality. They have painted concrete surfaces and wire nets, and are great for children learning the game or casual practice, but unsuitable for serious play. There is, however, no charge for their use.

Dining

Undoubtedly the main attraction at Apple Valley is the dining room, a comfortable, friendly place that exudes informal western atmosphere. Oil paintings of such famous desperadoes as Black Bart, Bat Masterson, and Jesse James adorn the dark paneled walls, and huge frontier-style light fixtures hang from the beamed ceiling. These are pleasant surroundings and the good food, good service, and very reasonable prices all deserve a gold star.

On Sundays, it is not unusual for six or seven hundred people to show up for the inn's regular hunt breakfast, with some coming from as far away as Los Angeles. This brunch is served from 8:00 A.M. until 3:00 P.M., long enough to spread out the crowd. It starts with a buffet of sumptuous fresh fruits, eggs, ham, sausage, chicken livers, and other breakfast fare in the morning, and at noon fried chicken and barbecued spareribs are added to the selection.

At lunch during the rest of the week, you can order sandwiches and other light fare, but most popular by far is the luncheon special, another buffet. If you choose it, it is best to do it in two trips. First, visit the well-stocked salad bar; then go back later for the sliced-to-order roast beef and other entrées. But beware: unless proper restraint is exercised, you won't be able to eat again that day.

At dinnertime (assuming forbearance at lunch), more good food is waiting. All the usual menu items are available, cooked and seasoned well, and at agreeable prices. The waitresses are attentive, adding a great deal to dining pleasure by bringing little niceties like cheddar and crackers to go with the wine before the main course, and tiny cones of sherbet to clear the palate between the salad and the entrée. All in all, dining adds up to a happy experience at Apple Valley.

Escape Ski & Racquet Club

Distances:
> From Los Angeles—130 miles; allow 3 hours
> From San Diego—141 miles; allow 3¼ hours

Features:
> Comfortable condominium living high in the San Bernardino Mountains; located at the base of the nearest major ski area to both Los Angeles and San Diego

Activities:
> Tennis, hiking, swimming, water-skiing and fishing on Big Bear Lake in summer; downhill skiing and other snow sports in winter

Seasons:
> Year-round; winter weekends from Thanksgiving to early April are usually booked up two or three months in advance; midweek and summer reservations are easier to make

Rates:
> $85 on weekdays and $100 on weekends for two-bedroom, two-bath units in winter; $75 and $85 respectively, in summer

Address:
> P.O. Box 1909, Big Bear Lake, California 92315

Phone:
> (714) 866-7504

Condominiums at the Escape Ski & Racquet Club

When the Escape condominium complex was built eight years ago high in the San Bernardino Mountains, it was conceived as—and has since proven to be—a resort for all seasons. Spring, summer, and fall are all pleasant times in this high country, with activities centering around Big Bear Lake, the tennis courts, and the pool. But its prime location right at the base of the Snow Summit ski area is the resort's true raison d'être. Winter guests staying in Escape's snug chalets are in the enviable position of being just a short walk from the slopes and their fine multilift system that attracts hundreds of thousands of skiers yearly.

Many innovative practices that have revolutionized the ski industry were pioneered at Snow Summit, in large part as solutions to some of the difficult problems that beset the area's founders. First, lack of natural snow through the fifties and early sixties nearly sank the project until its developers risked going into heavy debt to install the first large snow-making machinery in California. Fortunately it did the trick, and today, up to 95 percent of the runs are sometimes covered with artificial snow.

Other hardships—including drought, flood, fire, and a malfunctioning first chairlift—plagued the operation in its early days. The struggle to survive continued until finally, in 1973, a rare season of great natural snow increased income dramatically enough that more lifts and more snow-making equipment could be added. A period of rapid growth followed in which millions were spent on the lifts, new runs, buildings, restaurants, and all the services that comprise the present facility. Success led to a new problem, however—overcrowding—and once again innovative practices were pioneered at Snow Summit. The introduction of night skiing, controlled ticket sales, and a reservations system shrank the size of the lift lines and helped make this one of California's finest and most widely used ski areas.

So it is little wonder that the Escape complex next door is particularly popular, with skiers booking the chalets sometimes months in advance for many of the winter weekends. Fortunately, the pressures are reduced during the week, and all who can should try to arrange their getaways for midweek, when rates at Escape are lower and it is much easier to make reservations on short notice.

Routes and Distances

Only two hours and seven thousand feet separate the baking desert of Palm Spring's Coachella Valley from a world of snow, and green forests, and cool blue waters at Big Bear Lake.

From Los Angeles, drive east on Interstate 10 as if you were going to Palm Springs, but at San Bernardino turn north on Interstate 15E (not 15). Proceed about five miles on I-15E to the Base Line exit, which will put you on a crosstown freeway designated Highland Avenue/Mountain Resorts. Take this a short distance to another exit at a traffic light and bear left (east) on Highland Avenue, which becomes California 30/330. From here on the road rises steeply into typical mountain driving conditions. At six thousand feet, in the little town of Running Springs, Highway 330 ends. Take California 18 from there to Big Bear Lake. At the lake, continue to follow the highway along the south shore to Big Bear Lake Village. Go through the village, a long, drawn-out assemblage of tourist accommodations and shops, past a Jack-in-the-Box drive-in, just beyond which Highway 18 curves to the left. Continue to follow it to the first light. Make a right turn and remain on the highway to Summit Boulevard, which you will see just after passing a Kentucky Fried Chicken outlet. Go right on Summit to the base of the ski area, where you will find the Escape entrance sign on the left. This is a gated entrance: push the button, announce who you are, and the gate will be raised.

From San Diego, start out on I-15 until it branches just beyond Temecula and Rancho California into I-15E to the right. Stay on 15E into San Bernardino and look for the Base Line/Highland Avenue exit as described above.

Accommodations

The 130 condominiums at Escape, clustered on the hillside at the foot of the mountain, form virtually a village of their own. Fifty-five of these units are in a rental pool, with three basic designs available to the general public.

The first of these is the Olympic Model, a good choice for a couple or a party of four because, even though it is the smallest of the condos, it has two bedrooms and two baths. In this floorplan, the bedrooms and baths are upstairs with the living-dining area and kitchen on the main level.

For just a slightly higher rental fee, a larger party can reserve the Westridge Model, which is a split-level with two bedrooms, two baths, and a sleeping nook outfitted with either a trundle bed or bunk beds. The nook is ideal for children. Both it and the bedrooms are on the lower level, with the living quarters above. The final group, the Summit Condos, vary from the Westridge floor plan only in that there are three separate bedrooms and two baths on the lower level.

All of the Escape units are privately owned, and therefore varied in decor, but each is fully furnished and comes with certain basic equipment. This includes a fireplace, color television, patio furniture, and, in most units, a gas barbecue on the deck or patio. The kitchens are completely equipped and linens are supplied. Maid service is not provided unless you request it, but all linens are changed every three days.

The rates for the condominiums are based on a two-night minimum stay for weekends and three nights during holidays. A 15

The ski lifts are a short walk from the condominiums

percent discount is allowed for engaging a chalet for a full week any time except during the Christmas and New Year's holiday.

Rates are considerably lower midweek than on weekends, and the same is true of summer, which is off season here compared to the winter ski season. The management does make a special arrangement to help weekend visitors by cutting the price in half for Sunday night if they stay over. If it fits your schedule, this is a good way to avoid fighting the Sunday traffic going home. In all cases, a $50 security and cleaning deposit is required (which is returned if you check out with everything in good order).

Activities

During the ski season, condominium renters can buckle on their boots at home and walk over to the lifts to get an early start before the crowds arrive and while the snow is in prime condition.

The Snow Summit ski area is known for efficient operation. It has a total of eight chair lifts, two of them quads, which can transport thousands of skiers up the mountain. The longest chair, Number 2, is 5,475 feet long, with 1,150 feet of vertical drop. By using all these lifts, you can take fourteen miles of runs without once crossing your own track. Moreover, most of the runs are lighted for night skiing, which lasts until 10 P.M., and 11 P.M. on Saturdays and holidays. If nature fails to produce sufficient snow for good skiing, artificial snow-making machines are in place on all of the major runs to keep the area operating smoothly.

Ski schools and private lessons are conducted continuously for skiers of all abilities, rental equipment is available for anything you may have forgotten or don't have, and there is ample food service at several locations in the area. Lift tickets are not inexpensive; the standard adult tickets, good on all lifts all day, sell for $17.50, but there are other options for half days, night skiing only, and package plans that include instruction. An important thing to note about Snow Summit is its commendable policy of limiting ticket sales whenever anticipated crowds threaten to make lift lines too long. In order to make sure you will not be turned away and disappointed, you can make guaranteed reservations in advance (using a major credit card number) by phoning (714) 866-5841.

In addition to downhill skiing, there are places easily recognizable along the highway where inner-tubing and saucer coasting are popular and, at times when natural snow has fallen, there are good cross-country ski opportunities on the surrounding Forest Service trails.

The skiing activities usually come to a halt sometime in April, and the center of interest shifts to the lake and the tennis courts. The club's three well-kept, hard-surfaced courts are located directly be-

Skiing in the San Bernardino Mountains

tween the condominiums and ski lifts. It should be emphasized that it is important for those interested in playing tennis to engage a chalet whose owner is a member of the Racquet Club in order to insure court privileges. Fortunately, a high percentage of condominium owners do belong to the club.

There are no public bathing beaches on Big Bear Lake, so swimming opportunities are confined to the club's private swimming pool adjacent to the tennis courts. There are several marinas on the lake, however, where both fishing and water-ski boats and equipment can be rented. A launch ramp is available for anyone who cares to tow a boat up the steep access highway. For those who do, or who rent boats, the reward is reputedly fine trout fishing in the lake and excellent water-skiing on the smooth surface of its many secluded arms and bays.

Hikers have the run of the San Bernardino National Forest, which wraps all around Big Bear Lake and which contains innumerable Forest Service roads and trails to explore. The ski area also operates one lift during the summer for the benefit of sightseers. This is a good way to gain altitude fast and start your hike right among the summits of the San Bernardino Mountains.

Dining

The kitchens in every unit are modern and complete with all utensils and accessories, making it simple to do most of your eating "at home" while you are here. For the times when you want to eat out, there are a number of places to go within a mile or so of the condominiums. None of them is fancy or pretentious, and all have surprisingly reasonable prices. The closest is the T. J. Summit & Co. Restaurant, only a hundred yards away at the ski area. In winter, it throngs with skiers all day, serving regular skier's fast-food breakfasts and lunches until 3 P.M. Then it closes briefly for setting up and opens again at 5 P.M. as a dinner house. The dinner menus are limited to a half-dozen standard entrées: beefsteak, seafood, chicken, and so on, but it is good food and the atmosphere provides a relaxed and pleasant evening. A big stone fireplace with logs cheerfully flaming dominates one end of the room, and the decor is all related to skiing, with old-time skis, ski paraphernalia, and photographs hanging from the ceilings and covering the walls. Attached to the dining room on one side, and catering to its guests, is the small Polar Bar, while upstairs on the third level the much bigger Bullwheel Bar is heavily populated in late afternoons by the après ski crowd.

The T. J. Summit & Co. remains open during the summer season after the rest of the ski area shuts down. The View House, at the top of the one lift that continues to operate for the benefit of summer sightseers, serves a variety of quick foods, making a trip up the lift for lunch a pleasant midday outing.

There are also a few places in town you might like to try for dinner. The Iron Squirrel, about halfway up Pine Knot Street, is one of those generally recommended. (Go back the way you came on Highway 18 to the first traffic light, turn left, and you are on Pine Knot.) Across from the Iron Squirrel is Ronardo's, an Italian restaurant listing such items as jumbo shrimp for only $5.75.

A recently opened establishment that seems destined to become popular is "a Jewish-Italian deli and restaurant" (as it bills itself) with a French name, Château La Rue. You will find it in a little shopping center to the left off Highway 18 at Alden, just before you come to Pine Knot Street. It offers a large selection for breakfast and lunch as well as dinner in a typical American-Italian restaurant setting that is complete with lots of wine labels pasted on the walls and a profusion of Italian maps and travel posters.

Lower Desert *Getaways*

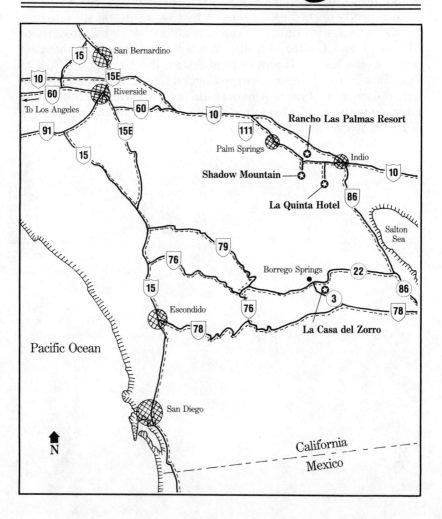

San Bernardino

Riverside

To Los Angeles

Palm Springs

Rancho Las Palmas Resort

Indio

Shadow Mountain

La Quinta Hotel

Salton Sea

Borrego Springs

Escondido

La Casa del Zorro

Pacific Ocean

San Diego

California

Mexico

N

Rancho Las Palmas Resort

Distances:

From Los Angeles—128 miles; allow 2½ hours

From San Diego—154 miles; allow 3 hours

Features:

Brand-new facilities designed from the ground up make this one of America's premier resorts, with every convenience; this big, lush establishment meets all expectations

Activities:

Twenty-seven holes of golf, twenty-five tennis courts, three swimming pools, therapy pools, bicycling, and evening dancing, all on the premises; Palm Springs shopping and other attractions just twenty minutes away

Seasons:

Year-round; wide variation in rates to encourage midsummer visits

Rates:

During high season (late December through mid-May) rooms are $140 to $155 for two people, and suites $225 to $350; in fall (September 18 to late December) rooms are $100 to $115, and suites $185 to $300; in summer (June through mid-September) rooms are $50 to $70, and suites $95 to $200

Address:

41000 Bob Hope Drive, Rancho Mirage, California 92270

Phone:

(619) 568-2727; toll free (800) 228-9290

Golf is a prime attraction at Rancho Las Palmas

If you were to start from scratch with a perfect site in a top resort area, no shortage of money, and the advice and know-how of dozens of experienced resort managers at your disposal, you might arrive at something very much like the Rancho Las Palmas. This is one of the newest operations of the Marriott Corporation, an experienced firm that operates over one hundred hotels worldwide. Drawing expressly on their experience with the famous Camelback Inn at Scottsdale, Arizona, they set out to build a luxury resort of the first order, and now, in its third year of operation, they have clearly succeeded.

At one time, the Coachella Valley in which it is located was all arid desert, except for the little spa town of Palm Springs at one end and the farming community of Indio at the other. Gradually, as water was brought down from the San Jacinto Mountains, a string of other settlements grew to fill the gap between: Cathedral City, Rancho Mirage, Palm Desert, and Indian Wells. The presence of water also led to a rapid proliferation of golf courses—there are now forty-three in the area. The towering San Jacintos serve another function: stoutly deflecting the smog and haze that sometimes hangs visibly in the distance beyond "windy corner" on the road to Banning.

Rancho Las Palmas is positioned at the center of the valley in Rancho Mirage within easy range of everything going on in the area—all the new restaurants, the new shopping districts, and of course the sunshine and golf courses. Like Camelback, it features sun, golf, and tennis, and unobtrusive personal service, which is always available wherever it is required.

With 348 rooms (soon to be augmented with additional construction), Rancho Las Palmas is already one of the valley's largest resorts, but it was cleverly designed to keep its size from being overpowering. Its activity centers are concentrated around two focal points where guests can easily see and be part of whatever goes on at the moment. Fanning out from the central lobby, for example, are two attractive restaurants, a variety of shops, and the main bar and lounge. Straight through the lobby is another outdoor restaurant with colorful umbrella-topped tables, and this in turn overlooks the main swimming pool, always alive with sunbathers. Just beyond the pool, where it is easy to watch from the terrace, are a water hazard, one of the greens, and a tee-off point on the golf course, with players constantly coming and going. Walk through the lobby and out onto the terrace, and you quickly have a good overall picture of what Rancho Las Palmas offers.

The other center of activity is five minutes away at the Country Club, accessible by a jitney service circulating regularly back and forth from the hotel. Here are another restaurant, bar and lounge, snack bar, and another swimming pool. There are also a golf pro shop, tennis pro shop, the first holes of the three golf nines, a putting practice green and driving range, plus all of the tennis courts. Here again, all facilities are concentrated so you can see and be a part of everything happening with just a quick, short stroll.

Routes and Distances

From Los Angeles, it is easy freeway driving all the way to Rancho Las Palmas. Start on Interstate 10, or take California 60 or 91 until you intersect with I-10, then stay on 10 through Beaumont and Banning and continue past the Palm Springs exit at California 111. Keep going on the freeway until just before Thousand Palms, where you take the exit onto Bob Hope Drive. Go five miles south toward the mountains on Bob Hope Drive, past the Eisenhower Medical Center to Rancho Las Palmas on the left.

If you want to go through Palm Springs, take the Highway 111 turnoff and stay on 111 through Cathedral City and most of the way through Rancho Mirage to Bob Hope Drive, which is well marked, and there turn left. Rancho Las Palmas is on the right, just beyond a new shopping center, soon after you enter Bob Hope Drive.

From San Diego, take Interstate 15 and 15E north to California 60, then go east on 60 to I-10 at Beaumont and proceed as above. If more time is available and you prefer a scenic route, get off I-15E at

Romoland and proceed east through the San Jacinto Mountains and the San Bernardino National Forest on California 74. You will emerge onto Highway 111 at the southeastern corner of Rancho Mirage. Go left on 111 about one mile to Bob Hope Drive.

Accommodations

Room selection is relatively easy because there is only one basic choice to make: either a regular room or a suite. All the rooms and suites have private patios or decks, which in turn are situated to view the golf fairways and greens. The slight variation in room prices is based on location; some rooms are considered more convenient than others.

The layout of rooms is always the same. They are large for hotel rooms, with space for a sofa as well as an easy chair and coffee table. They all have large baths with tub and shower, plenty of closet and drawer space, two double beds (or a king), a color television set, radio, and a telephone. Everything is new, clean, and carefully kept.

If you want lots of space or intend to entertain, take a suite. It is approximately twice the size of a room and, accordingly, costs about twice as much. It will have a king bed in an alcove that can be curtained off for privacy. The main room has several sofas and lounge chairs arranged for conversation, a wet bar, and a small conference table. The room can seat nine or ten people comfortably, and has a large patio running its full length. The bath is also very large and luxuriously equipped, with its own telephone, television, and even a bidet.

Activities

At the same time the Marriott chain decided to build their stunning new resort, they were able to negotiate an ownership position and management rights to the Rancho Las Palmas Country Club next door, thus acquiring a first-class golf and tennis facility they could make available to hotel guests.

If you are staying at Rancho Las Palmas, you have full membership rights at the club and can sign for expenses incurred there. A quick ride on an open-air jitney bus shuttles guests from one facility to the other. The Country Club is private, but if you elect to go over in your own car, presentation of a room key will get you through the guarded entry gate.

As the golf course is made up on three nines, you can vary your game by signing up for 1 and 2 the first day, 2 and 3 the second, and 1 and 3 the third. All the nines end up at the clubhouse, and an interesting innovation is the direct-line telephone at each ninth tee-off point from which you can call the snack bar and order sandwiches and beer to be ready for you by the time you finish putting. There is a big pro

The ranch's decor reflects Spanish influence

shop in the clubhouse, as well as a complete staff of teaching professionals for those who want a lesson. Greens fees at this writing are $22 for eighteen holes.

The tennis shop is in a separate building next to the golf shop, with the tennis courts adjacent. This is no small facility. There are twenty-five excellent, individually fenced tennis courts, eight lighted for night play, and one with grandstands for tournaments. Three competent pros are on hand to help with lessons, aided by a closed circuit videotape system for review and comment. Hotel guests can rent tennis courts for $6 per court hour.

A swimming pool and Jacuzzi at the country club are at guests' disposal, but for swimming and lounging, most find it more convenient to use one of the two larger pools close to their quarters at the hotel. Each of these also has a hot spa as well as an outdoor hot dog stand and a small bar serving exotic cool drinks.

A good way to see the immediate neighborhood is by bicycle, and the management thoughtfully has made complimentary bikes available. The preferred way to see the desert, however, is on horseback. The concierge in the lobby will make arrangements for you through the Smoke Tree Stables in Palm Springs.

One of the things that sets Rancho Las Palmas apart is the length to which its staff and management go to make their guests feel at home and at ease. Most weekenders arrive on Fridays, so every Friday evening the general manager holds a reception on the Fountain Court Terrace, with complimentary cocktails, a mariachi band, and a sumptuous array of hors d'oeuvres. All management personnel and newly arrived guests are invited so they can mingle and get acquainted. On Sunday afternoons another complimentary affair is held, this time a high tea to which the hotel's guests are again invited.

One more unusual feature of this resort is the Caravans Desk located just off the lobby. Here, a knowledgeable employee will make suggestions for those looking for something to do and will also make all the arrangements for whatever outing is chosen. It might be a shopping trip to Palm Springs, a tour of one of the valley's date farms, a trip up to the top of Mount San Jacinto on the aerial tramway, or any of a dozen other intriguing possibilities.

Dining

For most vacationers, dining out each evening is the highlight of the day. Rancho Las Palmas is twice blessed, because it not only has several excellent in-house restaurants, but is situated practically in the heart of the desert's famous "restaurant row," where many of the finest dining establishments in California are clustered.

The sophisticated Cabrillo Room at the Rancho is one of the newest of the elegant restaurants to become a part of this distinguished group. Its setting is a thoroughly delightful early California style—high beamed ceilings and polished tile are a backdrop for antique buffets, high ladderback chairs around tables draped with starchy white linen, and walls covered with memorabilia and pictures of bygone days in California history. It all makes for a pleasant spot to

Guests dine at the Fountain Court

relax and listen to the soft music of strolling guitarists and almost incidentally to enjoy award-winning continental cuisine. Each evening, the chef prepares a special creation, which the waiter will describe, in addition to the extensive regular menu. Everything is à la carte in the Cabrillo Room and, as you would probably expect, not inexpensive.

The Cabrillo Room is open only for dinner, but directly next door is the less formal Fountain Court Restaurant, which serves all three meals, starting at 6:30 A.M. each day. The Fountain Court is popular and nearly always abuzz with activity, and its prices are somewhat more moderate than those in the Cabrillo Room. True to its name, this thoroughly delightful room is a real courtyard, with a fountain and green tropical plants.

The third in-house restaurant is the Sunrise Terrace, a large outdoor area overlooking the golf course, and probably the most popular place to eat during the day. It serves breakfast and lunch buffet style, with a wide assortment of colorful, tempting dishes that lure swimmers and loungers from all directions to enjoy a meal at leisure under one of the bright umbrella tables.

An integral part of the food-and-drink operation is Miguel's Bar, located between the two restaurants and positioned to serve drinks on the terrace as well. It features live entertainment and nightly dancing. You can hear the music faintly from the hotel lobby, inviting a closer visit.

For those who would like to know their food costs in advance, Rancho Las Palmas offers an American Plan for all three meals at a flat $37 per person (in 1982). This plan excludes the Cabrillo Room, however.

After exhausting the local possibilities, you can ask the concierge at her desk in the lobby for information about the many other restaurants in the area, and she will make reservations if you wish. The chapter in this book on Shadow Mountain describes some of the authors' preferences among other places to visit in the area.

Shadow Mountain

Distances:
> From Los Angeles—130 miles; allow 2½ hours
> From San Diego—156 miles; allow 3¼ hours

Features:
> This is a medium-sized, fully staffed tennis resort 14 miles south of Palm Springs, with attractive grounds in a compact, conveniently arranged layout

Activities:
> Tennis, tennis classes and clinics, swimming, Jacuzzi spa; all the Coachella Valley's desert attractions, the El Paseo shopping district, and many golf courses are nearby

Seasons:
> High season runs from mid-December through May, fall season is October to mid-December; resort remains open in summer, but with minimal services

Rates:
> High season, $55 to $100 for two people, $160 for one-bedroom condominiums; fall season, $45 to $90 for two people, $140 for condominiums; summer rates available on inquiry

Address:
> 45750 San Luis Rey, Palm Desert, California 92260

Phone:
> (619) 346-6123

Studio condominiums open directly to the pool

In recent years, most of the old, established resort hotels in the Palm Springs area, where you could take rooms for a short time at a reasonable cost, have gradually disappeared. One after another, their owners have discovered the financial delights of "going time-share," or otherwise selling off rooms and apartments to investors who form a private club of the property and thereby close it forever to the general public. The newer hotels that have been replacing them tend to be large, impersonal, and expensive.

Shadow Mountain is a standout exception to this trend and therefore of increasing popularity with those wanting to visit the desert for a few days at a time, play lots of tennis, have a room that opens onto the swimming pool, and not be charged a fee for everything they do.

It is true that Shadow Mountain's living units are all privately owned, but these owners are typically people who use their properties for a week or two each year and the rest of the time keep them in a rental pool managed by the resort's central office. From the public's point of view, it operates like a hotel and has the advantages of a hotel. You check in, check out, make reservations, and use credit cards exactly as you would at a hotel. One notable difference is that, being privately owned, the units have more individual character, and the upkeep standards are higher than those sometimes found in strictly public establishments.

Started in 1947 as a golf and tennis resort, Shadow Mountain is one of the oldest continuously operating establishments in the valley. Only its objectives have gradually changed, with the emphasis being shifted from golf to tennis, so that this is now one of the top-ranked tennis resorts and teaching clinics in the country. It should be noted, however, that this is an all-round resort, and in no way restricted to tennis players. It sports the biggest figure-eight-shaped pool we have seen in our travels, and the pool area and adjacent lawns swarm with people swimming, basking, or reading in the shade of the many neighboring trees.

A cross-section of Shadow Mountain visitors during the season proves its popularity by the proportion of regulars who come back every year. Their loyalty is assured by the relatively low prices for rooms and food and the free, unlimited use of the tennis courts, and also by the resorts' central location in the valley, its handsome grounds, and the accessibility of its facilities.

Routes and Distances

From Los Angeles, Interstate 10 is the road to the Coachella Valley. Start out on I-10, or take California 60 to where it intersects with I-10 at Beaumont, or take the southern freeway, California 91, to Riverside, where you switch right onto 60 and then onto I-10.

From Beaumont, go eighteen miles farther on I-10 to the Palm Springs Highway, California 111, and follow that to Palm Desert. A quicker way is to stay on I-10 for another fifteen miles to the plainly marked Palm Desert turn-off at Bob Hope Drive. Take Bob Hope Drive south through Rancho Mirage, back to Highway 111, and go left on it a short way to Palm Desert. Halfway through Palm Desert, look for San Luis Rey Road. Go right there one-half mile to Shadow Mountain Resort on your left.

From San Diego, go north in I-15 and 15E to the intersection with California 60 near Sunnymead. Go right on 60 to Beaumont, pick up I-10, and proceed as above.

Accommodations

Like most resorts that have developed in stages over the years, Shadow Mountain has a variety of rental units differing considerably in size and character. When the resort was opened, the original guest quarters were in what is now referred to as the "Y" building, which flanks the swimming pool and is close to all the other activities. The lower units of this two-story building have sliding doors opening directly onto the lawn and swimming pool are just a few yards from the tennis courts and pro shop.

The upper units each have their own decks overlooking the scene. For reservation purposes, these are all called studio condominiums, and we consider them to be the best choice for a couple planning to spend a short time, such as a few days or a week. These units are a bit unusual in layout. They are large, long, narrow rooms that have all been remodeled in the last few years. In the daytime they are furnished like living rooms; at night they are converted into bedrooms by pulling down a large Murphy bed from the wall. Each one has a small kitchen, including a refrigerator, several burners, and a dishwasher. All utensils are supplied, making it convenient to fix breakfast or lunch, or even dinner if you care to eat in.

For longer stays, and if you want something more elegant—at higher prices, of course—many beautiful new condominiums have been built in clusters around the perimeter of the resort. These all have a basic core of living room, dining area, and kitchen complete with breakfast bar, and one bedroom and bath. Adjoining bedrooms with individual baths open off either side. These can be closed off to rent separately as hotel rooms, or opened up to make the condominium into a two- or three-bedroom unit. If two or three couples come together and take one of the big units jointly, it makes a very economical and comfortable way to go. Some of the condominiums are a distance away from the tennis courts and pool, so request one of

Full-sized condominiums can be rented

the closer ones if proximity is important to you.

The individual bedrooms, which of course have no cooking facilities, are the least expensive units at Shadow Mountain. Next in price are kitchenette units, which are rooms located behind the "Y" Building, furnished with a king bed and a tiny kitchen. The "Y" units are next on the price ladder, with the full condominiums at the top. Convenient parking is available for all units.

Activities

Shadow Mountain now has sixteen top quality, individually fenced tennis courts, four of them lighted for night play. Its tennis program includes free clinics from nine to ten each morning for anyone interested in brushing up, and a full-time tennis director who arranges games and competition for anyone without partners.

The head tennis professional is Leoncio Collas, known as a "pro's pro," and responsible for devising and setting up the teaching programs at several established tennis camps, including the famous John Gardner's. For the past six years he has been doing the same thing at Shadow Mountain, which is now ranked among the top fifty tennis resorts in the country by *Tennis Magazine*. Leoncio and his assistants give private lessons and put on the daily free clinic. They also conduct two intensive teaching programs each week called the Desert Tennis Clinics, one for two days and one for four days. The cost is $50 per day and the clinics are limited to Shadow Mountain guests. Each clinic session commences at 8:30 A.M. with a continental breakfast and ends at 4:00 P.M. after five solid hours of teaching. The level of instruction and intensity is on a par with John Gardner's, Vic Braden's, and other top tennis camps, making the Shadow Mountain program one of the best bargains in the country.

Golfers used to be able to play right next door at the Shadow Mountain Country Club, but that is now private, and the resort has made arrangements for its guests at the Rancho Las Palmas' twenty-seven-hole course in Rancho Mirage. The greens fees there are $25; the front desk will make tee-off reservations and provide transportation to the course for those without automobiles.

Palm Desert is a half-hour from Palm Springs, which is well known for all the diversions it offers visitors. Smoke Tree Stables, for instance, located at the southern end of town, has a fine string of horses available at $10 per hour for riders who want to get out into the unspoiled desert the old way, on horseback. Then there is the world-renowned aerial tramway to the top of the San Jacinto Mountains, where on a clear day the view of the Coachella Valley is absolutely spectacular. The Desert Museum and the Indian Canyons, sites of the palms and springs from which the town took its name, are

Shadow Mountain has the largest pool in the lower desert

worth individual visits, and the shops along Palm Canyon Drive are a paradise for those who like shopping. (Closer to home, the new line of shops along El Paseo in Palm Desert is rapidly gaining almost as much recognition. Even if you don't want to buy anything, it is pleasant to stroll up one side of the divided street and down the other, window-shopping and mingling with the crowd.)

People who want to hike and see the desert on foot have an advantageous location at Shadow Mountain. The gateway to the Living Desert Reserve is no more than three-quarters of a mile south on Portola Avenue, which runs along one side of the resort. The Reserve is a 900-acre park and garden with some three miles of self-guided nature trails, an aviary, and a botanical garden, all of which display living examples of the flora and fauna natural to the desert.

Dining

Shadow Mountain's own restaurant is The Top of the Court, located above the pro shop, where it has a commanding view of the pool and tennis courts. It serves all three meals: breakfast from 7:30 to 12:30, lunch from 11:00 to 2:30, and dinner from 5:30 to 9:30. Both breakfast and lunch can be had outdoors on the sunny deck, from which it is fun to watch the activities all around while you eat.

The evening menu at Top of the Court doesn't pretend to compete with those of all the elaborate dinner houses along "restaurant row" in Palm Desert and Rancho Mirage. It limits itself to ocean whitefish, New York steaks, fried chicken, and jumbo scampi, but its prices are eminently reasonable and what it does serve, it does adroitly and well. As one native told us, "It serves the best whitefish on the desert, don't miss it." Hamburgers and salads are also available, and on weekends there is a happy hour with complimentary hors d'oeuvres and entertainment in the early part of the evening.

When it comes time to try an alternative to Top of the Court, there is no end of possibilities. The desert is full of fine restaurants, but they are almost always crowded, so reservations are in order.

Here are a few of the good places close by. If you like Mexican food, try Las Casuelas Nuevas, notable not only for its excellent cuisine, but also for its elegant setting. Fans of Italian food have any number of choices, with The Nest and Villa Banducci's two of the best. For something really different, go to Mario's, where singing waiters regale their guests with operatic highlights and songs from popular stage shows.

La Cave and Entienne both serve authentic French cuisine and are dear in price, but offer true elegance and attentive service. For continental dining, go to Dominick's, or to The Cabrillo Room at Rancho Las Palmas, and for the best in American food try the new Medium Rare that serves the finest prime rib, steak, rack of lamb, and seafood at reasonable prices in its four intimate, pub-style dining rooms.

La Quinta Hotel

Distances:
  From Los Angeles—138 miles; allow 2¾ hours
  From San Francisco—494 miles; allow 10 hours
Features:
  An old-line resort with an international reputation for low-key, comfortable elegance, located in the desert nineteen miles south of Palm Springs
Activities:
  Golf, tennis, two swimming pools, bicycling, or strolling and relaxing on extensive, beautifully kept grounds
Season:
  End of September through May; closes down for the four hot summer months
Rates:
  $95 to $150 for two people for cottage rooms; $190 and up for suites; add $42 per day for American Plan meals
Address:
  P.O. Box 69, La Quinta, California 92253
Phone:
  (619) 564-4111; toll free in California (800) 472-4316; toll free outside California (800) 854-1271

Frank Capra still lives and writes in a La Quinta bungalow

Many of the grand resort hotels built in the 1920s as retreats for the rich and famous are gone now, existing only in the memory of a few remaining old-timers. But not so with La Quinta, one of the finest examples of the period. It has only mellowed with time and is operating today with the same graceful elegance and charm as when it was built in 1926.

The name La Quinta derives from a practice in the old Mexican army of marching hard for five days and then bivouacking for two to rest the men and horses. The troops looked forward to that fifth camp, or in Spanish, "la quinta," and the name still carries strong connotations of a happy sanctuary in which to relax and recuperate.

Walter Morgan, a millionaire from San Francisco, first became attracted to the Coachella Valley for his own La Quinta because of the warm winter weather, and he chose a "cove" near its southern end far back in the Santa Rosa Mountains to build a beautiful hacienda for his family, scattering a number of bungalows over wide lawns for the use of guests. Today the original hacienda is the core of the hotel, and the bungalows are part of the present guest quarters.

Everything was built with thick adobe walls, painted glistening white, and roofed with red tile in the Spanish manner. The hacienda was given a charming pillared front. Most of the materials were handmade, including the roof tiles, which were baked on the spot in a brick kiln.

Since Walter Morgan's time, there has been a series of owners who, fortunately, have maintained the property with loving care and, more or less, in its original state. In 1976 the Landmark Land Company acquired it with an ambitious plan for expanding and improving the original concept.

What they have managed to accomplish is unique because the program included the addition of one of the finest sports complexes in the nation without damage to the La Quinta charm and architectural integrity.

When a new dining wing was needed, for example, it was built as an addition to the old hacienda in such a way that it seems to be an integral part of the original structure. The same meticulous attention was applied to an elegant new tennis clubhouse, which is up to date in every respect and yet is actually a careful conversion of an early California ranch house already on the property.

The most impressive addition is the twenty-seven-hole golf course, designed by architect Pete Dye, who refused to have his imagination impeded by budgets or other arbitrary limitations. It is said that during construction two million tons of earth were moved to transform the terrain to his satisfaction, and already the results are being touted as the finest desert course in the world. Its lovely new clubhouse also reflects the original La Quinta flavor and is perched on a high mound to overlook the green fairways that extend like fingers into the desert and mountain canyons.

Despite all the innovation, La Quinta's aura as a private place to retreat from the world prevails, not just for the wealthy and famous, but for all who are willing to treat themselves to an elegant vacation.

Routes and Distances

La Quinta is nestled into its mountain cove at the lower end of the Coachella Valley, approximately nineteen miles southeast of Palm Springs. To get to it from any of the major cities, drive to Palm Springs, then continue on California 111 through Rancho Mirage, Palm Desert, and Indian Wells to Washington Street, a major intersection. Go south on Washington Street a mile to Eisenhower Drive, then go right again. Follow the drive for another mile to the La Quinta Hotel sign on the right.

If you come down Interstate 10, you can save time and bypass Palm Springs by continuing on the freeway until you come to the well-marked Washington Street intersection, just before Indio. Go south here and follow the instructions above.

Accommodations

La Quinta houses all its guests in the adobe bungalows randomly placed on the grounds. New structures have been added to the original cottages, but so carefully have the old ones been maintained and so closely do the new units imitate them in every detail that it is difficult to tell them apart. About the only distinguishing features of the newer units are desert sand rather than white adobe walls and small ice-makers and wet bars that are handy for those who plan to entertain.

No matter which cottage you stay in, the chances are it has been occupied in the past by famous guests. The Duke and Duchess of Windsor, Ike and Mamie Eisenhower, Bette Davis, Greta Garbo, Errol Flynn, and a host of others all favored La Quinta when they came to the desert. Today, Frank Capra, the well-known film director, now retired, still lives in one of the bungalows where in the past he wrote such well-remembered screenplays as *Mr. Deeds Goes to Town, You Can't Take It With You,* and *Lost Horizon.*

Most of the bungalows are designed as triplexes and fourplexes, in which each room has its own separate entrance and covered patio, with the rooms interconnected so they can be opened up to form suites when necessary. There are a few single and double cottages, as well as several large compounds built in Spanish style around a central courtyard.

All told, there are some 170 individual units, all of them spacious, with thick adobe walls that guarantee quiet, slatted wooden shutters for privacy, and baths with both tubs and stall showers. The rooms are comfortable and are furnished with excellent taste. Most have fireplaces, which at first seems incongruous in the desert, but can be a real boon when temperatures drop dramatically when the sun goes down.

Activities

A large staff of gardeners keeps La Quinta's grounds groomed and bright with the color of a thousand flowers, oranges, and grapefruit in bloom or fruit all under a canopy of lofty date palms. A network of pathways connecting the cottages and activity centers passes through these gardens, so that walking and exploring the grounds is one of the most pleasant activities here. You will also see people stretched on chaise longues in front of their cottages, sunning or reading, and for many visitors these quite pursuits, plus partaking of the good food and an occasional dip in the pool, are all the activity they want or need.

Farther up the active list are bicycling and jogging, which the relatively flat terrain of the valley floor encourages. Precedent for the latter was established by no less a personage than Burt Lancaster, whose habit was to come to La Quinta to get in shape for one of his typically vigorous movies. Employees like to recount seeing his familiar figure jog by in the early morning during these visits.

The golf course extends into desert and mountain canyons

Nevertheless, golf and tennis are what the majority come for. There are many fine golf courses in the Coachella Valley, some made famous by such well-known players as Dwight Eisenhower and Gerald Ford, and it is not easy to make comparisons; but there is no question that the new course at La Quinta ranks near the top. Already the Southern California Golf Association has put it among the four toughest courses within their jurisdiction. More than fifteen hundred palm trees line its fairways, with four lake hazards, a profusion of pot bunkers, and challenges like the sixteenth hole, which is surely destined for fame in the golf world. With no fairway at all, it presents 170 yards of rocky scree between its high tee and the lonely target green far below and craftily bordered by traps. The lush verdancy of this whole course is accentuated by the backdrop of dry mountains rising right from the fairways and forming spectacular scenery for every hole.

The clubhouse is nearly as dramatic, set on its commanding knoll and encompassing a full pro shop, dining room, and bar. The golf clubhouse is about a five-minute drive from the hotel. The greens fee for hotel guests is $40, which includes a cart rental.

La Quinta's tennis facilities are closer to the hotel, just a minute's walk away, and are set up as a private club which extends membership privileges to hotel guests for $12 per day per player. Like the golf club, the tennis facility has a handsome clubhouse with pro shop, restaurant, and bar, plus a pretty swimming pool. Two teaching pros

The tennis clubhouse and championship court

are on duty and will help set up matches for people who want competition. Breakfasts and luncheons are served at poolside or on a terrace overlooking the sunken championship court. Charlie Pasarell is the full-time tennis director, and is usually active about the premises where guests can meet him and exchange a few words about the game. Arthur Ashe, Bob Lutz, Stan Smith, Tom Gorman, Roscoe Tanner, Marty Reissen, Dennis Ralston, and other well-known pros also take particular interest in this club and can often be seen around the courts. They have a project in mind, now well advanced, that will make La Quinta a major tennis center attracting national tournaments and top-ranking players. The facilities available include four fine grass courts, a stadium court capable of seating eight thousand specators, a sunken championship court, and twelve night-lighted, hard-surfaced courts clustered around the clubhouse. Watch La Quinta: we expect it is destined to become one of the tennis world's best-known names.

Dining

Guests now have the option of an American Plan for meals, which includes breakfast, lunch, and dinner at one basic rate, or the regular European Plan, where all meals are optional. "Restaurant row" in Rancho Mirage and Palm Desert is not far away, so if you enjoy venturing out for an occasional dinner or luncheon, the regular plan will probably be to your advantage.

All dinners at La Quinta are served in the main dining room. Breakfast and lunch can be taken there, too, or at the tennis club or in the golf clubhouse.

The dinner hour is a special time. Guests usually dress up a bit for the occasion and plan to spend a leisurely time enjoying themselves in the lovely old-world atmosphere of the dining room. The high, beamed ceiling, graceful archways, and white adobe walls of the large room make a perfect setting for the many sparkling tables, each with a colorful floral arrangement, fresh each day. (The resort employs a full-time flower arranger just for the purpose.)

The menu is unique. Decisions must be made about the entrée, but not the price. One price covers everything, which always includes an appetizer, salad, soup, the entrée, dessert, and beverage. The price is not low, but there are few complaints because every detail of the meal is beautifully prepared and seasoned. A good variety of meat and seafood dishes is offered, the wine list is excellent, and a group plays soft music for listening or dancing.

La Quinta is famous for its Sunday champagne brunch, which draws crowds from all up and down the valley each week and which recently received a special award for excellence from the Southern

California Restaurant Writers Association. It is served outdoors on the terrace, buffet style. You will be overwhelmed by the endless choices and by the huge mounds of chilled king crab and roast beef—and circulating waiters keep the wine glasses full.

The daily luncheon in the dining room is also an elegant buffet, but on a more modest scale. For an informal lunch, which you can have in tennis clothes or swim togs if you want, nothing is more pleasant than to eat outdoors under an umbrella at the tennis club, where you can watch the action on the sunken championship court from your table. An equally good choice is lunch at the golf clubhouse, which also offers an informal setting. Or, if you plan to be out on the course, the clubhouse will pack a box lunch to stow in your cart.

La Casa del Zorro

Distances:

From San Diego—90 miles; allow 2 hours

From Los Angeles—160 miles; allow 3½ hours

Features:

An old, small, pretty oasis in a little-known section of desert; serves good food and charges reasonable rates; a friendly and welcoming atmosphere

Activities:

Swimming, tennis, outdoor badminton, ping-pong, shuffleboard, putting green, desert hiking, and bicycling (if you bring your own bike); eighteen-hole championship golf course nearby

Seasons:

Year-round, but still relatively undiscovered in summer

Rates:

$50 for studios, $60 for suites, $75 to $140 for houses for two people, October through May; $35 for studios, $40 for suites, $50 to $90 for houses, June through September

Address:

P.O. Box 127, Borrego Springs, California 92004

Phone:

(619) 767-5323

La Casa del Zorro or "the home of the fox"

Old-timers like to tell how Borrego Springs today resembles the Palm Springs of thirty or forty years ago. Both are desert oases, but where Palm Springs has grown and proliferated into a sprawl of condominiums, resorts, and satellite towns, Borrego Springs is still a small community only just stirring with signs of development. Separated by twenty-eight miles of desert from the nearest town to the east and ringed by dry, treeless mountains on the north and west, it is still very much isolated from the outside world.

It seems paradoxical, given this isolation, that Borrego Springs is only a two-hour drive from San Diego. The real mystery to people who love the area is how it managed to resist growth for so long and remain relatively undiscovered. All that may change one day, but meanwhile, when you arrive at La Casa del Zorro for the first time, you cannot help feeling you have made a discovery and hoping that you will be the last one to share the secret.

La Casa del Zorro, Spanish for "the home of the fox," is five miles from town on the Yaqui Pass Road. It is an old establishment, originally built as a ranch when the total population of Borrego Springs was just twenty-five souls. Over time, the ranch proved more viable as a stopping place for friends and travelers than as a place for raising cattle and gradually converted to a way station that became known as The Desert Lodge. During those years, it developed a limited and very select clientele from San Diego society: people who valued privacy, a low-key pace, the dry air, and, above all, the fragile beauty of this little-known portion of desert.

Today, the original ranch house remains as the central lodge building, its staunch adobe walls constructed by Indian laborers using traditional methods. The original adze marks are still clearly visible on the hand-hewn rafters that were once soaked in fish oil to preserve them.

The dining room, kitchen, offices, and Fox Den Bar are all located in this building, which is now surrounded by many flower gardens and low buildings containing studios and suites, as well as eighteen individual cottages. There is an inviting swimming pool near the entrace and the tennis courts are just behind, sheltered by a row of hardy tamarisk trees. Inside, the ranch house welcomes its guests in a big, traditional sitting room filled with comfortable furniture arranged around a fine old stone fireplace. The walls are covered with original western paintings, complements to a second large collection in the dining room, which together are an early-American art buff's dream.

The art, the little resort, and the town of Borrego Springs each merit a visit, but the real attraction is the spectacle of the desert itself, full of color and strange shapes, and always changing with the light. On maps, the town appears as a white patch in the midst of a green, roadless expanse labeled Anza Borrego Desert State Park.

Dry air and fragile beauty in the remote desert

Most people envision deserts as flat, sandy expanses broken only by rippling dunes, but that is seldom the case. This desert has its flat areas, but they are gouged by deep, precipitous canyons; rising directly behind the town is the high, beautiful rampart of the Santa Rosa Mountains, once the despair of early pioneers crossing in search of promised lands of rich farms and gold.

You cannot help trying to imagine the hardships and trials of those times and sympathizing with the hardy people who made that trek as you drive the fine paved roads that lead over the mountains and through the Anza Borrego Desert. It is an experience you will not soon forget.

Routes and Distances

From the San Diego area, drive east on Interstate 8 to El Cajon, then go north on California 67 to Ramona. At Ramona, pick up California 78, which takes you through towns with the picturesque names of Santa Ysabel, Witch Creek, and Scissors Crossing. After Scissors Crossing and a lot of very scenic mountain driving, look for Road S3 on the left, also known as the Yaqui Pass Road. Take S3 for approximately six miles to the junction with Brawley Road, where you will see La Casa del Zorro on the right.

From Los Angeles there are a number of ways to go, but the quickest is to drive south to Anaheim, then take California 91 to Corona, and there switch to Interstate 15 to Temecula. At Temecula pick up California 79 through Aguaga Valley to Warner Springs. Continue a few miles past Warner Springs to the power station, turn left on Road S2, and follow it to Scissors Crossing. At Scissors Crossing go left again on California 78 to the Yaqui Pass Road, S3, and Casa del Zorro. Note that coming from either San Diego or Los Angeles it is not necessary to go through the town of Borrego Springs, which lies approximately five miles north of the resort.

If you approach from the east, from Indio or El Centro, take California 86 along the west shore of the Salton Sea to County Road S22. Go west on S22 for twenty-eight miles, past the Borrego Springs airport, to the Borrego Valley Road. Go left there, follow it around by Rango Way to the Yaqui Pass Road, and look for Casa del Zorro just beyond the next intersection.

Accommodations

The guest accommodations are generally quite delightful and, although they vary significantly in size and shape, they all share the advantages of convenient parking close by and a good deal of privacy.

Lodgings range in size from small studio units to three-bedroom, three-bath houses. Thirty-four accommodations in all provide something to fit just about every need.

There are no longer any guest quarters in the ranch house proper. The studio units and suites are consolidated in three one-story buildings across the drive from the ranch house and quite close to it. The individual houses are widely spaced, scattered at random all over the property, with their own little yard areas and patios or porches for outdoor lounging.

All of the units have been recently redecorated, each house with a different motif. The houses range from one to three bedrooms, and are most livable and an excellent value. All have nice living rooms, kitchens or kitchenettes, and patios that provide desert views. The smaller houses are perfect for a couple who want the luxury of extra space and privacy. The larger ones are good for family groups, and the biggest ones, with a separate bath for each bedroom, are ideal and inexpensive for two or even three couples vacationing together and sharing costs.

The individual units are most appropriate for short visits by single couples. The studios are furnished with two studio couches, which convert to beds at night, while the suites have small sitting rooms and big bedrooms furnished with one king or two queen beds. Both have private baths, of course, and private patio areas outside sliding glass doors. All the rooms and houses are provided with color television sets.

Activities

La Casa del Zorro is open year-round, but there is a wide variation in the people who come and what they do in the different seasons. In the winter, when days are balmy and temperatures hover in the seventies, the "snowbirds," as employees jokingly call them, flock down from the north and even from Europe to escape the cold and snow. In the summer, however, when temperatures sometimes exceed 120 degrees, most of the visitors are from San Diego, people who slip over to bake in the sun and "dry out."

At either time of year, the one facility always in use is the swimming pool in the lawn next to the ranch house. With its unusual eighteen-sided shape, palm trees right at water's edge, and bright flowers cascading from surrounding raised beds, it is one of the prettiest pools we have seen. On hot summer days, poolside is the place to read and sun between dips and perhaps have a drink from the Fox Den which opens to the pool. That is about the extent of outdoor activity.

In winter, the pool is still the focal point of the inn, but there is a lot more going on. The two tennis courts situated behind the sheltering tamarisks have excellent surfaces and good lighting for night play. They are available for guests' use at no charge on a first-come, first-served basis. Courts are kept locked to prevent misuse, but the control system is simple. You trade your room key for a court key when you go out to play, and trade back when you are through.

Back of the ranch house, near the tennis courts, are layouts for other diversions, including a badminton court, shuffleboard, tetherball, and two ping-pong tables under a sheltered patio area. Right outside the dining room is a smooth, beautifully kept eighteen-hole putting green of carefully cropped Bermuda grass.

Regular golf has traditionally been a favorite spring, winter, and fall sport here. In the past, guests have always been welcome at the DeAnza Golf and Country Club in Borrego Springs, but now that is changing. A brand-new eighteen-hole championship course under construction practically next door to the inn, at Ram's Hill, is scheduled for completion in the fall of 1982. Guests of the resort will play there in the future, and play at the DeAnza Country Club will be restricted to members.

As we have mentioned, the desert itself is always the prime attraction here, and if you can bring bicycles they provide a marvelous way to explore the quiet back roads and experience desert scenery that is hard to see any other way. The alternative is hiking, and for that there are numerous trails through the Santa Rosa foothills. Just where Palm Canyon Drive dead-ends north of Borrego Springs is a visitors bureau, part of the Anza Borrego Desert State Park, where information about trails and weather can be obtained. It is advisable to check in and out here when undertaking long hikes. A twenty-minute slide show depicting the history and ecology of the Borrego desert shows continuously and is well worth the trip to see.

Dining

Many fine meals have been served in the two adjoining dining rooms of the old ranch house since La Casa del Zorro became a full-fledged resort back in 1960, and its reputation for good food has increased steadily ever since. All three meals are served daily—indeed, this is a necessity, because there are very few places to dine in the area, and none of them nearby. Happily, in spite of its near monopoly, the inn has always maintained high standards of quality and service while charging reasonable prices.

Its two dining rooms are the Presidio and Butterfield Rooms, each designated by an ornate sign over its doorway. The thick white adobe walls of both rooms are covered with the collection of original artwork that the inn's owner has acquired over the years. This is not a random collection, but concentrates on one theme, the exciting early days of California history, and most of the paintings were done in oil on specific commission by the well-known artist Marjorie Creese Reed. Her primary subject is the Butterfield Overland Stage, which connected the

Original Western art is featured in the dining room

Far West with St. Louis in 1858, two years before the Pony Express reached San Francisco. Your dinner in the dining room becomes an exciting tour of scenes that took place over the Butterfield route through this very section of desert during those formative times.

In both dining rooms, an unusual custom-loomed carpet from Ireland featuring rich tones of green, blue, and red forms an elegant background to tables covered with starched white linen. The atmosphere is not formal or stiff, but since there is little else to do in the evening, dining is an occasion, and gentlemen are requested to wear jackets and ladies a dress or evening suit. Dinner specialties include steak, prime rib, and seafood, as well as several exotic Polynesian dishes. A wide selection of fine wines is available, as well as cocktails from the Fox Den Bar next door. You can look forward to friendly service and leisurely dining here.

Middle South Coastal
Getaways

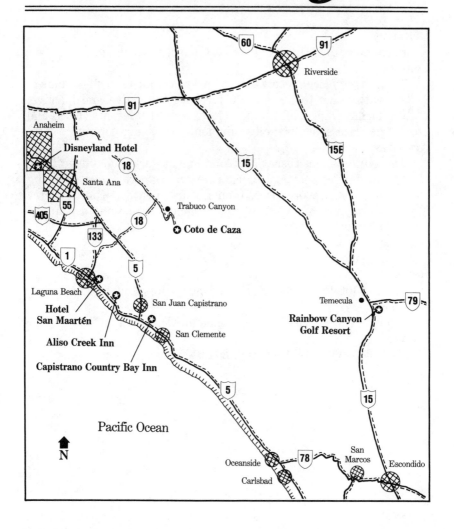

Disneyland Hotel

Distances:
From downtown Los Angeles—28 miles; allow ½ hour
Features:
This is a very large resort hotel complex, completely self-contained, with much to see and do for both the active and inactive; facilities include a wide selection of restaurants, bars, and delicatessens; live entertainment is provided nightly
Activities
The world-famous Disneyland Amusement Park is next door; three swimming pools, gardens, a replica seaport, and a shopping mall on the premises, tennis courts nearby; Knott's Berry Farm and many other Los Angeles attractions are in the vicinity
Seasons:
Year-round
Rates:
$94 to $106 for rooms for two people; suites $140 and up
Address:
1150 West Cerritos Avenue, Anaheim, California 92802
Phone:
(714) 635-8600; toll free (800) 854-6165

The Disneyland Hotel and the Seaports of the Pacific bazaar

The need to get away is really a need for a change of scene and change of pace, and for most this automatically means leaving the city for the solitude of the country or the seacoast or some equally different environment.

But it would be a mistake to forget the old saw about "getting lost in a crowd." The Disneyland Hotel is right downtown, but its size and scope and the very number of people it attracts are so large that the hotel operates on an impersonal basis and you are assured of the kind of relaxation that comes with anonymity.

Indeed, it is the exact opposite of the cozy inn where everyone makes a point of knowing everyone else and trying to remember names. You can be as alone as you want to be here—in this luxurious environment that swirls with activities you can participate in or observe from the sidelines, as your mood dictates.

The hotel itself occupies fully sixty acres of grounds in the city of Anaheim, and, although it connects directly with the Magic Kingdom of Disneyland, it is a separate entity and offers a surprising variety of fantasies in its own right.

The main components of the hotel are three sleek, separate highrise towers arranged on three sides of a landlocked artificial marina known as the Seaports of the Pacific. Exotic ports of call from Mexico, Hong Kong, and Australia have been recreated in detail, each with its own fascinating shops and restaurants and little bars on the wharves, all authentic down to colorful peddlers hawking wares along the quay. There is even a fairly large mall on the property, with more interesting shops for gifts and necessities, additional restaurants, and a nightclub.

In the evening, the resort takes on a different character. Shafts of narrow, multi-colored laser beams are projected from building to building, piercing the darkness above the seaport and aerially intersecting to create a spectacular art form. When you tire of watching the lasers, you can stroll down through sunken tropical gardens below a colorfully lit waterfall that drops into a pond full of golden carp. You can also walk along the white sands of a palm-studded Papeetian beach and listen to music coming from one of the wharves where the entertainment goes on nightly.

In short, daytime or evening, there is always more to see and do, with so much of it utterly unique that it is difficult to compare this hotel with any resort we have visited. Most people enjoy it thoroughly; a few may find it a bit overpowering, but we have met no travelers who didn't consider their trip to the Disneyland Hotel a fascinating experience.

Colored laser beams are a nightly light show

Routes and Distances

Nothing is simpler than getting to Disneyland. From either north or south, take Interstate 5 to Anaheim and watch for the sign for the Disneyland exit. (The white peak of the Matterhorn and the spires of various other exhibits are visible from the freeway and give ample warning you are approaching Fantasyland.) A few short blocks from the exit, with the way clearly marked, you will enter the gate of the huge parking lot for the amusement park. Tell the attendant you are destined for the hotel, and a pink slip will be placed on your windshield. Thereafter, other attendants along the way will wave you on to the hotel's check-in facilities.

Your room may be in any of the half-dozen buildings surrounding the central "seaport." A bellman will escort you to an appropriate parking area and then help take your luggage to the room. The hotel parking fee is $2.50, which you will pay upon leaving.

Accommodations

The hotel complex contains a total of 1,150 rooms, mostly in the three tower buildings, but some in a scattering of motel-like villas located about the grounds.

Whoever first conceived of this project must have been a person of large imagination and undaunted ambition. Who else could have imagined such exotica as the seaport, waterfall, and all the other dazzling attractions intermingled with the business of running a large hotel? And it is a business that is expertly run. Despite its size and the thousands of people who mill about the premises, the buildings, grounds, and rooms are always neat, clean, and meticulously maintained.

The rooms themselves, except for the suites, are much alike, varied mainly by the different views and the size and number of beds. All rooms are air-conditioned and spaciously arranged, with comfortable and attractive furnishings—as would be expected given the rates charged.

People who want even more luxury can get it by taking one of the penthouse suites on the eighth floor of the Bonita Tower. There, they will have several balconies with expansive views, two baths, a wet bar complete with refrigerator and stools, a big separate living room, and two television sets. This is a roomy, comfortable layout for anyone expecting to entertain family or friends.

From any of the rooms it is but an elevator ride and short walk to all the attractions and restaurants on the grounds, and for those who desire, no more than a ten-minute walk to Disneyland itself.

Activities

All the world knows that the Magic Kingdom, Fantasyland, and

Disneyland are one and the same, and that at least one visit in a lifetime to the Mecca of the West is practically mandatory. For many making this pilgrimage, the Disneyland Hotel, which is connected to the grounds by continuously circulating free trams and a bullet-shaped monorail, is the perfect base from which to make the tour. The uninitiated should be warned, however, that Disneyland can be little more than glimpsed in a single day, and to see it all and do everything will take closer to two full days. Various kinds of tickets are available, with possibly the best value represented by the Passport ticket, which costs $10.25 and covers both general admission and unlimited use of all facilities (except the shooting galleries).

The name Disneyland is so ubiquitous that the uninformed are apt to think the hotel and the amusement park are parts of a single entity, but they are not, and it is not at all necessary to visit the park to have a good time. There is plenty to do right at the hotel. On its grounds are three swimming pools, one of them Olympic-size, with lanes for doing laps; the two others are adjacent to the Tahitian beach, where swimmers can take the sun on the white, palm-fringed sand. For youngsters, there are paddle boats to rent in the marina, and tennis players are invited to use the ten night-lighted courts (for a fee) at the nearby private Tennisland Club.

The most fun for young and old alike, however, is probably just

Disneyland's pirate ship still draws the crowds

strolling around the property among the buildings, looking at the sights, browsing in the shops and exhibits, and "people watching" the other guests, who are doing the same. For people are everywhere, in and out of the International Artisan's Bazaar, inspecting the boats and boutiques along the waterfront, having beverages at the Wharf Bar, sampling wines and cheeses at the Wine Cellar, or watching the carp in the ponds by the waterfall. When you tire of that and want to go farther afield, information is available from the activities director in the lobby about what there is to see in greater Los Angeles and how to get there. The *Queen Mary* (owned by the same people who own the hotel), Knott's Berry Farm, Marineland, or the various Hollywood studios are only a few of the endless possibilities available nearby.

In the evenings, both before and after dinner, you find a bit of unusual nightlife at the new Sergeant Preston's Yukon Saloon, where you will be impressed by the effort that has been expended to create an authentic 1898 gold rush atmosphere. The costumed waiters and bartenders frequently break into spontaneous bawdy song, and the customers, who are quick to catch on, join in the choruses with much clapping and hooting. Outrageous contests and surprise entertainments punctuate the fun. Drinks are moderately priced and include free pretzels and other nibbles.

From Sergeant Preston's you can move on to the wharf, where there will be more music and entertainment. You can dance to a live western-style band in one of the spots, listen to jazz piano in another, or have a nightcap at the little nautical bar over the water. Even if you never leave the hotel, you'll find innumerable diversions.

Dining

Selecting a place to dine at the Disneyland Hotel is no easy matter, since there are as many to choose from as you will find in most medium-sized towns. All the restaurants are handily clustered on the mall and wharf, but each has its own characteristic cuisine and specialties.

The Shipyard Inn, for one, on the wharf overlooking the marina, has a reputation as one of the finest seafood restaurants in an area known for good seafood. Its luncheon specialty is oyster stew, and at dinner time the heavy favorite is a hearty cioppino.

You will find a completely different atmosphere in the Oak Room, where a warm English Tudor decor creates the ambience of a private club—which, in fact, it once was. The attentive service is reminiscent of those club days, and its menu offers a variety of continental cuisine. Those partial to veal will be faced with an agonizing choice when deciding between expertly prepared veal piccata, veal marsala, and veal chanterelle.

El Vaquero, the hotel's fine Mexican restaurant, is right in the center of restaurant row and is well known for the special treatment it gives steaks and seafoods, using chili peppers and other Spanish spices. Its steak picado and swordfish pio pico are representative of the finest early California cooking.

Not all the restaurants are formal dining rooms. Margie's Pantry, for example, is a sidewalk cafe in the heart of the complex. It has outdoor tables where you can enjoy freshly baked croissants with coffee, or one of their crepe or quiche specialties. Another is the Chef's Kitchen, which serves all three meals, buffet style, and is especially noted for its salads and tempting desserts. The nearby Coffee House is the perfect place for a quick snack: it specializes in sandwiches and hamburgers, and also serves three meals a day.

Finally, the favorite fast-food spot is probably Señor Campos, back out on the wharf. Those with a taste for Mexican food will be delighted by the selection of tacos, enchiladas, burritos, and Mexican pizzas.

Coto de Caza

Distances:
From downtown Los Angeles—60 miles, allow 1¼ hours
From San Diego—89 miles; allow 1¾ hours
From San Francisco—495 miles; allow 8½ hours

Features:
A place for active people; big, comfortable, informal; located in one of California's many sunny canyons, and home of Vic Braden's world-famous tennis college

Activities:
Tennis, western and eastern horseback riding, all shooting sports, hunting, basketball, volleyball, bowling, two swimming pools, racquetball and handball, exercise room and saunas

Seasons:
Operates year-round; tennis college sessions start at 8:30 A.M.: Saturday–Sunday (2 days), Monday–Wednesday (3 days), Monday–Friday (5 days)

Rates:
Rooms and suites range from $70 to $125 for two people; tennis college is $175 per person for 2 days, $300 for 3 days, and $400 for 5 days

Address:
P.O. Box 438, Trabuco Canyon, California 92678

Phone:
(714) 586-0761

Coto de Caza's condominiumlike accommodations

Located in the southeast corner of Orange County just over an hour from Los Angeles, Trabuco Canyon runs away from the coast deep into the foothills of the rugged Saddleback Mountains. The farther you drive along the twisting road into the canyon, the more remote the scene becomes, until finally you enter into a virtual tunnel of dense live oaks spreading from either side of the road. Then suddenly you emerge into a beautiful, serene valley, where handsome estates with barns, board fences, and horses grazing in the meadows around them dot the hillsides. This is the entrance to Coto de Caza, a place deceptive in its apparent tranquility, since this is also where the action is.

It is true that sometimes you want to go on vacation just to relax and "do nothing," but sometimes it is stimulating to go where you will be actively engaged, physically and mentally, to return home with new ideas and objectives. Coto de Caza is that kind of place.

The name Coto de Caza means "hunting estate," which is how the place began. Hunting and shooting on its several thousand acres of upland meadows and hills, in season, are still an important part of the program, but the heart and soul of the resort are now the famous Vic Braden Tennis College. Tennis buffs from all over the country—or the world, for that matter—come here to eliminate the faults from their game under the tutelage of probably the most famous and certainly the most affable professional in the business.

This resort also boasts one of the finest and largest equestrian centers in the West, with every conceivable kind of training, teaching, and showing facility. It has the kind of gymnasium, workout room, and swimming pool necessary for Olympic athletes to train, plus strictly recreational facilities as well, such as bowling lanes, racquetball and handball courts, Jacuzzi spas, and extensive children's playground equipment.

Despite the resort's overall size and scope, most of its activities are arranged compactly and conveniently around a central building known as The Clubhouse. The Clubhouse contains the check-in counter, dining rooms, and cocktail lounge. Off the lounge is a patio overlooking the Olympic-size pool, and directly adjacent, connected by a broad, lattice-sheltered deck, are the gymnasium, locker rooms, and indoor athletic courts. The elaborate tennis college layout is on the far side of the deck, and next to that is the Coto Sports Research Center, where Vic Braden's staff applies scientific analysis to the development of new teaching techniques. Behind the tennis college are the tennis courts themselves, with a footpath leading past the courts to the townhouse-like groups of guest lodges that are arranged in staggered rows on a wide meadow. The lodges, designed very much like condominiums, contain an even hundred rental units and have another, smaller recreational pool and spa centrally located among them. People walk easily from their rooms to The Clubhouse, but there is also a perimeter road for automobile access to the General Store and Equestrian Center an eighth of a mile from the lodges, and the Hunt Club, the most distant facility, three miles back in the hills.

Routes and Distances

The little town of Trabuco Canyon is located in the canyon of that same name, some sixty miles south and east of downtown Los Angeles and approximately fifteen miles north of San Juan Capistrano. The town occupies the lower end of the canyon; Coto de Caza fills all the upper end. To get to it from either north or south, driving on Interstates 5 and 405, the San Diego Freeway, look for the El Toro Road exit (Country Road S18). Take this exit and drive east on El Toro Road, past the El Toro shopping center, to Live Oak Canyon Road at Cook's Corner. Go right on this road, past a large recreational area called O'Neill Park, to the Coto de Caza entrance, about twelve miles from the freeway. The entrance has a guarded gate; once you tell the attendant who you are it will be raised quickly. It is three more miles from the gate to the Clubhouse.

The closest airport to Coto de Caza is the John Wayne (Orange County) Airport, about thirty-five minutes driving time away. The resort sends a van to the airport every Wednesday, Friday, and Sunday evenings to drop off people checking out of the tennis college and pick up newly arrived "students."

Accommodations

When you stay at Coto de Caza, you will be put up in a group of guest lodges, fifty-four of which are staggered along the perimeter road south of the tennis college. Each guest lodge is really a complete condominium or townhouse, with a main living room, kitchen, dining area, bedroom, and connecting second and third bedrooms, the latter usually upstairs on the second floor. The upstairs rooms can double as small apartments, each with its own bath, balcony, and separate entrance, so the entire unit can be rented as a whole, or the connecting doors locked and all parts rented separately, depending on each group's size and needs.

Spaciousness, comfortable furnishings, and tasteful decor can be expected in all these accommodations, which break down into five price categories, starting with what are called ranch rooms, the least expensive of the facilities. All the ranch rooms are located upstairs and consist of a bedroom furnished with two double beds, a bath, and a tiny balcony. Next on the rate card are deluxe rooms, which are also upstairs, but include a sitting area as well as the balcony.

The suites are just slightly more than the deluxe rooms, are not all

Instruction at Vic Braden's world-famous tennis college

upstairs, and have the added advantages of a wet bar and a refrigerator.

Loft rooms, the fourth category, include a bedroom with two
queen beds, a wet bar and refrigerator, a balcony, and a sitting area
with a sofa that makes into another bed.

Finally, there are the master suites, the core units on the lower
level around which the other rooms are grouped. These have a big living room, dining area, kitchen, master bedroom, and private outdoor
patios.

All the units at this resort have the advantage of individual
covered parking spaces for guest automobiles directly adjacent to
their entraces. Coto de Caza is strictly informal, and there are no
doormen or bellmen to contend with. You check in at The Clubhouse,
drive to your room, and move yourself in. Ice is available in several
close locations for everyone without refrigerators. All rooms have
televisions and digital clock-radios (so no tennis college students will
have an excuse for missing the early class!). Food supplies for those
with kitchens can be purchased at the General Store, and everything
else is within easy walking distance.

Activities

If you want to see a group of slam-bang, hyperactive athletes
working out, this is the place to do it—especially when the U.S.
Women's Olympic Volleyball team, whose official training base is Coto
de Caza, are at practice in the gymnasium. Coto de Caza was also
chosen as the site of the 1984 Modern Pentathlon, the grueling sport
in which entrants must excel and compete in each of five separate
events: swimming, running, shooting, fencing, and riding.

These athletes all come to Coto de Caza for one thing, the unique
assortment of facilities available to them. These include the gymnasium, exercise and workout rooms, the Olympic-size pool, pistol and
rifle ranges, the big equestrian center, and miles of cross-country
trails. The great thing for us ordinary mortals is that these are all
available to us, too, not to mention Vic Braden's Tennis College.

The gym where the women work out by day is a standard basketball court open for pick-up games in the evening. Right beside the
gym, along its length, is a little two-lane bowling alley with automatic
pinsetters, and clustered at its end, next to The Clubhouse, are the
two handball and racquetball courts, free for the use of guests. There
are also elaborate men's and women's locker rooms, each with a row
of showers, sauna baths, and "hot box" suntan rooms, and next to
them a mirror-walled unisex workout room containing weights and a
complete Universal gym. Even the big Olympic-size pool, laned for
competitive swimming, is a dual-purpose facility, with The Clubhouse

bar and terrace on one side and plenty of lounge furniture for sun-bathers and recreational swimmers scattered on its other margins.

During Coto de Caza's early days, riding and shooting were the focal points around which it developed, and although they have been somewhat overshadowed since by the tennis college and athletic facilities, they still represent an important and unique facet of the operation. Today, the equestrian center is a very elaborate complex of barns, indoor and outdoor riding rings, corrals, bleachers, stables, and acres of covered paddocks for visiting horses. Every May the big-gest, most prestigious horseshow in the West takes place here with an impressive array of both western and eastern competitive events and judgings. During the balance of the year, youthful riders can be seen training daily in the rings. Guests of the resort can rent horses and take riding lessons or go for guided trail rides on some thirty miles of trails into the surrounding back country.

Riding at Coto de Caza, in other words, is a serious sport fully im-plemented with first-class facilities. The same can be said of the Hunt Club, in its isolated location three miles up the valley from the resort proper. There, around the rustic clubhouse, its pretty dining room and broad terrace shaded by a famous nine-hundred-year-old oak, are a skeet range, a standard eight-station trap range, and two unique, highly useful innovations for shotgunners, the "duck shoot" and the "crazy quail." The former is a trap house set high on a steep hill with the shooting station below, so that the birds flying straight overhead perfectly simulate action in a duck blind. The latter is a series of traps hidden along a path through a canyon, so that birds jump out unex-pectedly as the shooter proceeds along the trail.

For formal target work, on the other side of the clubhouse are ranges of twenty-five, fifty, and a hundred yards for those shooting pistols or high-powered rifles. You can rent a shotgun for the clay-bird shooting, but should bring your own piece for use on the ranges. The resort also runs a shooting school for novices, with professional in-structors who furnish revolvers and automatic pistols as part of the curriculum. The shooting school is run by appointment, so inquiries should be made in advance for those who want to attend.

Finally, but most important of all, is the Vic Braden Tennis College. You can register for two-, three-, or five-day sessions of exciting, inten-sive, scientifically designed basic instruction in the game of tennis.

If you decide to come to the college, here is what to expect. The first day, check in between 8:30 and 9:00 A.M. for registration and fill out an experience form that will classify your degree of skill and enable you to be assigned to the appropriate class. Then your photograph is taken on the court as you stroke a tennis ball. (An 8 × 10 print will be presented to you on graduation, "to keep you humble.")

Jumping practice at the resort's equestrian center

Next is a short movie on tennis and a brief orientation, followed by Vic Braden himself, who comes running in clutching a racket and ball, and proceeds to stimulate everyone (classes typically run from forty to sixty students) in his typically humorous style. Serious fun. He explains the basis of his teaching system, which the students are going to practice and which every instructor faithfully follows throughout the session.

After that, you go out on the courts and hit about a thousand balls a day. The groups are small, never more than six per instructor, and each group goes from court to court on a carefully planned schedule, with a different instructor at each station who drills you on a specific fine point of the forehand, backhand, volley, serve, or smash. In between the court sessions, you will go frequently to the automatic hitting lanes to practice grooving the strokes that you have learned.

Each morning session lasts from 9 A.M. until noon, with an "orange break" in the middle. Then an hour and a half for lunch, and you are back on the courts for another three hours, until 4:30 or 5 P.M.. Some people want to work longer. An instructor is on hand for them, and ball-throwing machines are available until 9 P.M. in the evening.

The second day and each one after will follow essentially the same format, but will progressively introduce new material while continually brushing up on the earlier instructions. During the routine, Vic himself will pop in and out, occasionally taking a hand in the instruction. The rest of the time he busies himself in the Coto Research Center, doing computerized studies of human motion—specifically, on how athletes can better use their bodies to improve their output, whether it is in furtherance of a golf swing, tennis stroke, long jump, discus throw, or whatever else is available for study. In the end, because tennis is his game, he manages to relate whatever he learns back to tennis and to incorporate it into the college's curriculum.

Dining

The informal spirit that prevails at Coto de Caza carries over to the dining. The main dining room is just off the lobby of The Clubhouse, adjacent to the Wagon Wheel Saloon, and serves three meals a day to guests as well as to residents of the surrounding Trabuco Canyon community. In order to attract the continuing business of these residents, who tend to be a discriminating group, every effort is made to keep quality standards high but prices in the reasonable range, all of which works in favor of the Coto de Caza guests.

The room itself is warm and comfortable, with walls paneled in mellow, rough-sawn wood and with a massive fieldstone fireplace. High-back wicker chairs give the individual place settings a sense of privacy, augmented by little hurricane lamps on each table that cast subdued lighting. Guests dress casually here; no one comes to dinner in tennis or other athletic attire, but jackets and ties are not required.

The dining room menu is not extensive, but always has several meat and fish entrées, with a different special every night in each of these categories. The regular dinner includes a trip to a very nice salad bar and individual loaves of homemade bread. In addition to the main entrées, a number of light supper selections are available, and are a boon for those with small appetites and those counting calories. These include items such as soup and salad bar dinners and steak sandwiches.

Once a week dinner is served at the Hunt Lodge up in the valley. During the cooler months, the entrée is always an excellent prime rib of beef, served inside, in a small area that can only hold about fifty people, so early reservations are important. In summer it is held outside on a deck under the great, ancient oak tree. At this time, the menu is changed to informal barbecues and specialty dinners, and many more guests can be taken care of.

Breakfasts at Coto de Caza are in the main dining room, and tennis garb is permissible then. Regular lunches are also available in the dining room, but for tennis players and students at the tennis college, lunch is in the adjacent Garden Room which is a bright, cheerful, skylighted area full of green plants, both inside and outside in the garden courtyard. As the tennis players stream in, they are greeted by big trays of cold lemonade and iced tea, and their choice of a hot or a cold buffet, spread out elegantly at the end of the room.

A popular alternative for lunch is the old-fashioned soda fountain at the General Store, a ten-minute walk from The Clubhouse. The treats include genuine chocolate sodas and other old-time favorites, and thick beef and pastrami sandwiches (one sandwich split between two people is often enough) that can be eaten at the fountain or on one of the tables outside, looking out over horses grazing and the Saddleback Mountains in the background.

For dinner away from the resort, Trabuco Oaks Steak House near Cook's Corner is only a five-minute drive away. It is fun and funky, and serves good steaks cooked over an oak-chip fire. To illustrate how informal it is, anyone who enters wearing a necktie has the tie promptly cut off with scissors, or is at least warned this will happen. It is probably true, because there are actually hundreds of cut ties hanging from the ceiling beams, and photographs in the entry of such luminaries as a smiling Richard Nixon submitting to the scissoring. There are a few other passable places to dine farther out of the canyon toward the coast, but this crazy steak house is one you don't want to miss.

Hotel San Maartén

Distances:
> From Los Angeles—55 miles; allow 1 hour
> From San Diego—66 miles; allow 1¼ hours

Features:
> Not yet well known, Hotel San Maartén is a delightful hideaway right on the main street of Laguna Beach; you can eat and swim in a sunny courtyard and never go outside; friendly, personal attention is a hallmark

Activities:
> Relaxing, reading, and napping in the sun; swimming in heated pool, use of saunas; strolling Laguna's famous ocean beach just a block away, browsing Laguna's shops and art galleries

Season:
> Open year-round; summer season is May 15 through September

Rates:
> $80 on weekdays and $90 on weekends for two people in summer; $64 and $72, respectively, in winter; inquire about retreat specials, sometimes available, which include dinner

Address:
> 696 South Coastal Highway, Laguna Beach, California 92651

Phone:
> (714) 494-9436

Laguna Beach's San Maartén Hotel

The San Maartén has been standing on the same corner on the main street of Laguna Beach for many years, but today it is a brand-new hotel. Complete renovation and remodeling a few years ago and, more recently, an overall policy change initiated by a new owner-management team, accomplished the metamorphosis. What some people may remember as a rather tired establishment has become one of Southern California's most delightful and least known hideaways.

The renovation was carried out by a former owner, who was so deeply impressed by the structures and landscaping he had seen on a trip to the Caribbean that he wanted to create a similar atmosphere in the hotel. He changed the name to San Maartén, after one of the islands, then began the extensive physical alterations. The artwork and the tasteful use of rattan and woven basketry intermingled with antiques carry out the Caribbean motif, but the influence is most apparent in the sunny courtyard, enclosed on all four sides but open to the sky. A profusion of tropical plants, including banana trees, a variety of palms, and exquisite ferns, creates a lush tropical atmosphere that can be enjoyed from every room.

This setting makes the hotel an especially desirable spot to relax and while away time, but what really raises it to its present quality is the thoughtful service rendered by all members of the staff, from the genial young manager to the newest busboy.

Our idea of a perfect getaway at the San Maartén is to park the car in the hotel's parking lot and never get in it again. You can spend most of your time lounging and reading by the pool, in the midst of the lush greenery. It is scarcely necessary to bestir yourself to have a fine lunch or even dinner since Gauguin's, the hotel's pleasant little restaurant, opens directly to the courtyard. Lunch is served alfresco in the garden alongside the pool, and dinner is also served outside on summer evenings.

The only excuse for leaving the premises is to cross the street to stroll on the beach or perhaps to browse in the numerous arts and crafts shops for which Laguna Beach is so well known. Otherwise, stay put at the San Maartén and follow the poetic advice of Walt Whitman: to "loaf and invite your soul."

Routes and Distances

Drive south from Los Angeles or north from Capistrano on California 1, the Coast Highway, to Laguna Beach. The Hotel San Maartén, halfway through town on the corner of Cleo Street, is easily recognizable by its red tile roof and surrounding palm and banana trees.

Accommodations

The San Maartén is a low, rectangular building constructed stockade-style around an open courtyard. Three sides of the building are two-storied, while one end has a third level where the hotel's four large suites are located. The other fifty rooms are located either on the lower level, which opens directly onto the pool and dining patio, or on the level above, connected by two stairways leading to a balcony that runs around the entire floor. All of the rooms on this level, as well as the office and lounge, open directly onto the balcony.

The hotel rooms are all spacious, with either a king bed or two doubles and a large dressing room and bath. But here the similarity ends, because each one is individually and tastefully decorated. Most of the furnishings are antiques, pleasantly mixed with rattan and newer pieces. Charming wallpapers and coordinated bedspreads, pretty lamps, and interesting pictures are effectively used throughout.

The rooms have telephones and televisions, the latter cleverly hidden in antique armoires. You will find also a vase of fresh flowers in your room if you arrive on a weekend, as well as two bottles of Perrier water and a bucket of ice.

Even though they are considerably more expensive than the rooms, the four suites on the third level are usually the first accommodations to be engaged. They are lovely indeed, with the living room furniture attractively and comfortably grouped around a fireplace. Each suite also has a small kitchenette and dining area, and a

Banana trees, palms, and ferns enclose the inner courtyard

bedroom, much like the regular units, furnished with antiques and prettily appointed. The baths, however, are unique, each with an enormous tub with Jacuzzi-type jets all around the sides.

Activities
We would guess that half the people who check into the San Maartén never leave the premises until time to check out. You don't come here for active sports, but rather to enjoy the good food, rest in the sun, and relax around the pool in its pretty garden courtyard.

Laguna Beach is known far and wide, however, as one of the West Coast's most interesting beach towns, so you may want to stroll the famous beach, or the town streets with their specialty shops and crowds of interesting people. A favorite walking trip is to go north from the hotel three blocks to Main Beach Park. From early morning to late at night this is a gathering place for young people playing beach volleyball and basketball, for artists doing curbside paintings, for picnickers, beer drinkers, and strollers of all sizes and shapes sporting every style of garb. If you continue to the end of Main Beach, you can climb the concrete stairs to Heisler Park, where a long, winding asphalt path leads along the cliff. The park is beautifully maintained, and is bordered on one side with attractive houses and apartments, and on the other by the ocean and beach. This is a favorite route for morning joggers, who can make a good run by going its length.

You can get a street map at the front desk of the hotel that lists points of interest, including the galleries and malls. One interesting walk is to go up Forest Avenue, opposite Main Beach, which is lined with shops, then cross over and come back down Broadway. From there, go out to the beach and walk back to the hotel along the waterfront. Then, to cap the day, you can relax in one of the hotel's saunas, each with a shower, located on the second-floor gallery above the courtyard.

Dining

If your plan is to get away on the weekend, try to time your arrival at the San Maartén to make the Saturday champagne brunch in the courtyard (from 11 A.M. to 3 P.M. on Saturdays and Sundays). It starts with a glass of champagne, and you will note that every glass is set precisely on a single red rose petal that reflects the color up the stem (this is the restaurant's distinctive trademark). A basket of hot cinnamon croissants and blueberry muffins comes with this first glass of champagne. Next comes a fruit platter, then your choice of quiche, omelet and other egg dishes, or louis, together with all the champagne you wish. The picturesque setting, where you can pick a table in the sun or the shade, encourages taking plenty of time to linger over the meal so you relax quickly into a vacation mood.

On warm evenings the courtyard tables are set again, so you have the choice at dinnertime of eating indoors or out. The food here is exceptionally good, and a sous-chef sees that it is attractively arranged. Gauguin's has only been open for a short time, but we think it is probably the best place to dine in Laguna. It has already received a Newcomer's Award as best new restaurant in Southern California. The indoor dining room is divided with plants and half-partitions to provide privacy and intimacy. Starchy white tablecloths, candles, and a fresh rose decorate every table—and again, you will find a single rose petal under your wineglass. The walls are all decorated with large, individually lighted Gauguin prints, which carry out the Caribbean theme in an otherwise dimly lighted room. Live piano or guitar music is a nightly feature. You will find dinner prices for fare ranging from red snapper to rack of lamb surprisingly reasonable.

The restaurant serves lunch every day, but the only breakfast is complimentary juice, coffee, and croissants in the hotel lobby. You may want to take a three-block walk south to Poor Richard's Bakery on the corner of the Village Fair mall for breakfast outdoors. It is a popular place, and you will see why when you taste some of its assorted freshly baked pastries. You can select your favorite, take it out with a cup of coffee to one of the little sidewalk tables, or because these are often occupied, sit on the curb or the wall while you eat.

If you want a change of pace for dinner, the place that currently has the best reputation in Laguna is the Partners' Bistro on the highway, just before you come to Main Beach—an easy walk from the hotel. The Partners' Saloon is just across the street from the Bistro; if you've found one, look across and you will find the other.

The liveliest restaurant and watering hole in Laguna is the big, ornate Las Brisas, perched on a headland overlooking the ocean at the south end of Heisler Park. If you are a "people watcher," don't miss Las Brisas for a drink during the cocktail hour, just to see the action. The food is Mexican-American and is almost as popular as the drinks.

Coffee and croissants at the nearby village bakery

Aliso Creek Inn

Distances:
From downtown Los Angeles—57 miles; allow 2 hours
From downtown San Diego—64 miles; allow 1¼ hours

Features:
A quiet, reasonably priced golfing resort located in a cool, narrow canyon a short distance from the ocean; each room is very private

Activities:
Golf, use of swimming pool, whirlpool spa; Aliso Beach State Park and Laguna Beach nearby

Seasons:
Year-round; May 20 through September 15 considered summer season

Rates:
$60 to $88 for two people in summer; $55 to $72 in spring, winter, and fall

Address:
31106 Coast Highway, South Laguna, California 92677

Phone:
(714) 499-2271

The unusual scalloped pool is surrounded by living units

By turning off the Coast Highway into the narrow Aliso Creek Canyon, you enter, in just a matter of yards, what seems a whole different world. The temperature is noticeably cooler, often a good fifteen degrees below that prevailing in the surrounding hills. Suddenly the roar of the highway is blocked off and a mantle of quiet falls over the surroundings. In the mornings when you awake, the loudest noise will be the plaintive call of the mourning doves that populate the canyon in surprising numbers.

The people who come here are mostly golfers who enjoy playing a relaxed, low-pressure game. In the summer season, after school is out, most families come for a full week, which the children spend playing in the pool or going out to the beach while the adults get in some rounds of golf.

Aliso Creek's most attractive features are its reasonable prices and its privacy. You may come with a golfing group and enjoy the conviviality of playing and partying together, but if a couple wants time to themselves, to read and rest and do their own thing, the arrangement and layout of the inn work well for that, too. All the accommodations are large, with well-furnished living rooms that invite you to relax in your own quarters. Since every unit has a kitchen, you are not dependent on restaurants, either, and can make coffee or get a cold drink from the refrigerator whenever you wish.

Best of all, each unit has a private fenced patio area with lounge furniture for outdoor living, and right off the patios of most units, through individual gates, is the pool and hot tub area, with more lawn furniture, umbrella tables, and a number of shade trees to sit under. Parking areas or individual carports are close to every unit to make moving in and out easy, and the golf course, beach, and restaurant are all within easy walking distance.

The history of Aliso Creek goes back twenty-five years. The golf course was built first, and how they squeezed it in between the canyon walls is a mystery, but the results contribute much to the charm. The restaurant came next, built by Ben Brown, whose family still owns the whole complex. The restaurant standards were high from the beginning, which, combined with the attraction of the golf course, lured people who wanted to come and stay for longer than a day. This finally led to the construction of the inn itself and to completion of the resort as it is today.

Routes and Distances

California 1, the Pacific Coast Highway, runs right along the beach at the point where Aliso Creek flows into the ocean and the Aliso Creek Canyon cuts back into the hills. To get to the resort from the north, drive south on Highway 1 two miles from downtown Laguna Beach. Come down a steep hill, and when you see the Aliso Beach Park ahead, with a concrete bridge crossing the creek at the bottom of the hill, do not cross the bridge but instead move into the left turn lane. You will then see the sign to Ben Brown's Restaurant to the left. Turn there, and drive three hundred yards to the resort.

Coming from the south on Highway 1, six miles beyond the junction with Interstate 5 at Capistrano, you will come down another steep hill to approach the southern end of the bridge at Aliso Beach Park. Cross the bridge and turn right at the Ben Brown sign.

Accommodations

Aliso Creek runs through the middle of the resort property and divides it in two, so that there are buildings on both sides connected by a bridge. Of the sixty-three total accommodations, an even dozen of the newest ones, called studio units, are on the far side of the creek across from the office, restaurant, and swimming pool. These are the most compact and least expensive rooms the inn has to offer, although each has 570 square feet of floor space, which is spacious by most standards. Each has a carport, a large combination living room–bedroom furnished with twin studio beds, a dressing room, a separate, fully equipped kitchen, and either a balcony or a patio.

Two different types of accommodations are situated on the near

Latticework and shrubs screen guests in the hot-spa

bank of the creek. The single-story units on this side are designed to provide spacious and comfortable quarters for a couple (over eight hundred square feet) and are only slightly more expensive than the studios. In addition to a separate bedroom furnished with either a king or two double beds, these units have spacious dressing areas and more closets than most people have at home. The large living room, comfortably furnished with a couch and easy chairs, also has a separate dining area with a pass-through to a large, fully equiped kitchen. A cathedral ceiling and windows under the eaves reveal the high green walls of the canyon outside, making the units seem even larger. Sliding doors lead from both the living room and the bedroom onto individually fenced patios. Each patio has outdoor lounge furniture, and a gate opening directly onto the common lawn, pool, and hot spa area.

A third type of accommodation at Aliso Creek also fronts on the pool area. These are two-story units, particularly popular with families or golfing foursomes traveling together. By sharing a unit, which has over eleven hundred square feet of space, two couples can save on room costs without being cramped. Downstairs are a large living room and dining area, a fully equipped kitchen, a half-bath, and a patio. Upstairs are two bedrooms, a balcony, and a full bath. All units at the resort have telephones, televisions, and daily maid service.

Activities

Golfers seem to enjoy the short, snappy, nine-hole course at Aliso Creek. Twice around is only 4500 yards, par-64, but it is a challenging par to make—interesting to play, but not overpowering. It is also a pretty course, with the canyon walls rising steeply on all sides providing shelter from the wind and summer heat.

Most people carry or pull their clubs, but electric carts are available if you want one. The cost of golf is eminently reasonable, at only $7 for eighteen holes on weekdays and $9 on weekends. Yet, it is a full-service operation, complete with pro shop, teaching professional on duty, driving range, and putting green. A snack bar and Ben Brown's well-known restaurant and lounge are right next door.

A ten-minute walk down the road along the creek brings you to the highway, and just on the other side is Aliso Beach State Park, one of the finest and best known of Southern California's many fine ocean beaches. To get to it, cross the bridge over Aliso Creek to its south side and find the pedestrian tunnel under the highway that leads directly onto the beach. There are restroom facilities, a public outdoor shower, a snack and ice cream bar, and a long, high fishing pier, all available for public use. In the early morning you can have this long beach pretty much to yourself, but it can get fairly crowded by noon on weekends.

The inn itself has a fine heated pool with unusual scalloped edges,

Aliso Beach, a short walk from the resort

set in a lawn ringed by the living units. It has a diving board at one end, and to the side is a large wading pool for children. Near the pool on a cabana deck is one of Aliso Creek's nicest features—a large whirlpool hot spa, enclosed with latticework and surrounded by a screen of flowering shrubbery to give those using it a sense of privacy.

Most guests at Aliso Creek enjoy making at least one excursion into Laguna Beach, just two miles north, to explore the interesting shops there that are filled with everything from fine antiques to funky beach wear. You can also stop at one of the pastry shops along the main thoroughfare of town and choose a sample from their tempting displays to enjoy with a cup of coffee at an outdoor table while you relax and watch the world go by.

Dining

Every unit at the inn has a large, modern kitchen adequate for cooking any meal you choose. Most vacationers prefer to eat out at least some of the time, however, and the area is full of good places to go, Ben Brown's, right at the inn, possibly the best of the lot.

Having operated for many years in the same spot, Ben Brown's has a reputation among local people for good food. That reputation has been solidly authenticated by the Award of Excellence from the Southern California Restaurant Association for the past five years. The two favorite dishes mentioned by the latest survey team were the bouillabaisse and veal Oscar.

The restaurant, located on the upper level of the golf clubhouse, takes special pride in its spinach salad, which it claims many imitate, but none can duplicate. It serves breakfast, lunch, and dinner not just to golfers and guests at the inn, but to people from all over Orange County. On weekends it often regretfully turns away many who show up for dinner or the Sunday brunch. Certainly, Ben Brown's owes its success to its good food, reasonable prices, and informal setting.

Those making an extended stay at the inn may want to go exploring at the dinner hour, and there are numerous opportunities in every direction. San Clemente is just ten miles south along the Coast Highway, and Dana Point Harbor and San Juan Capistrano are even closer, and all have good restaurants. Laguna Beach is just two miles north, also with a variety of restaurants. Our favorite there is Gauguin's in the Hotel San Maartén, described in some detail in the chapter on that hotel. The chapter on the Capistrano Country Bay Inn describes some of the other restaurants in the area.

Capistrano Country Bay Inn

Distances:

From downtown Los Angeles—48 miles; allow 1¼ hours

From downtown San Diego—62 miles; allow 1¼ hours

Features:

Small, convenient, and pretty, this cozy inn is a perfect getaway spot or stopover for people traveling the coast

Activities:

Walking and jogging on the beach, observing the inn's unusual antique car collection, sight-seeing in San Juan Capistrano

Seasons:

Inn operates year-round; summer season is May through Labor Day

Rates:

$55 to $115 for two people in summer; $40 to $80 for two people in winter

Address:

34862 Pacific Coast Highway, Capistrano Beach, California 92624

Phone:

(714) 496-6656

The Capistrano Country Bay Inn—a vintage roadside inn of the '30s

The Capistrano Country Bay Inn is one of those old, classic establishments built by the side of the road in the early 1930s. It hugs the Coast Highway, as was the custom in those days; otherwise, the only thing separating it from the broad, sandy Capistrano ocean beach is a set of railroad tracks from whence the nostalgic whistle and clickety-clack of an occasional Amtrak break the night silence. Recent restoration inside and out has returned the inn to its original state of elegance, and its relatively small size is turned to advantage. The young manager says, "We try to look after the individual needs of our guests and make their stay pleasant, which is something you can't do in a thousand-room hotel."

The moment you enter the little office, you are welcomed by a cheery "hello" or "hi" from the resident parrot. When you are shown to your individually furnished and decorated room, you will find the welcome reinforced by a split of chilled champagne awaiting your arrival.

The inn's location halfway between Los Angeles and San Diego, little more than an hour from either city, makes it an ideal getaway spot or layover for those traveling the coast. Its proximity makes it easy for travelers to arrange to have time to linger, so guests tend to arrive early and depart late. It is a lovely place to relax, rest, and stroll on the beach in the afternoon, then have a leisurely continental breakfast the next morning and spend an hour or two reading or

This old "woody" will pick you up at the train station

catching up on correspondence on the secluded patios or decks before moving on.

Those on a getaway who want to leave everything behind, including the family car, can come on Amtrak and be picked up in style by a member of the inn staff at the station in San Juan Capistrano, just a few minutes away. If you come by train, you won't have any trouble recognizing your chauffeur, who will arrive in an old "woody" station wagon, vintage 1915, which is part of the inn's meticulously kept collection of antique autos.

Routes and Distances

From Los Angeles, take Interstate 5 (or the San Diego Freeway until it joins I-5) south all the way through the little town of San Juan Capistrano. On the other side of this village, almost at the beach, California 1, the Coast Highway, merges with I-5 in a tangle of ramps and cloverleaves. Leave I-5 there, watching for signs directing you to Capistrano Beach and to the Coast Highway. (These will direct you north on Highway 1 very briefly, then you will see the turnoff to where the Coast Highway heads south.) Proceed south on the Coast Highway for about a half-mile and look for the inn on the left side of the road.

From San Diego, go north on I-5 to the same clover leaf or, better yet, get off at San Clemente on El Camino Real, which runs into and becomes the Coastal Highway. Proceed north along the beach for about three miles to the inn, which will be on the righthand side.

The other way to get to the inn, and possibly the most fun, is on Amtrak. Several trains a day run between Los Angeles and San Diego, stopping at both San Juan Capistrano and San Clemente. Just let the inn know when you are coming and someone will be there to meet you.

Accommodations

When the Capistrano Inn was restored and renovated, each room was individually furnished in the style of a classic country inn. There are only twenty-eight rooms, but all face west and have sweeping ocean views.

The view is especially fine from the second-story rooms, which have lovely small balconies with railings entwined by brightly colored bougainvillea. Comfortable outdoor furniture makes these balconies a pleasant place to sit and read in privacy, or just watch the view.

Beneath the balconies are flagstone patios for each of the first-floor units. Dense juniper and other plantings separate and seclude the patios on each side, and in front there are beautiful flower beds in a fountain court.

The inn's rooms are not large, but have many useful and in-

The day begins with continental breakfast on the balcony

teresting features. In addition to a large king or queen bed, the rooms have antique dressers, a table and chairs, a wet bar with a small refrigerator, and marvelous old-fashioned overhead fans. The piece de résistance is a hooded gas-burning fireplace, lit with just the strike of a match. This will furnish a cheerful glow for breakfasts in bed or, in the evening, will help dispel the chill as you sip sherry from a decanter thoughtfully provided by the management.

Other small touches, such as a bowl of live African violets on the table, do much to distinguish these rooms from more ordinary quarters and contribute to a pleasurable stay at this unusual inn.

Activities

You can begin the day by having breakfast delivered on a tray to eat in bed in front of the fire, and then, when the sun is high, move outside to read, write, and watch the beach and the occasional passing trains.

If you want to join the constant parade of joggers and strollers, walk across the highway and the railroad tracks, step through a gap in the fence, and then jog on a path paralleling the beach. You can go north all the way to Dana Point, a good, long run. People also swim, surf, picnic, and hunt for coins in the sand with metal detectors here. You can do any of these, or simply watch others doing them.

If you are interested in old cars, you can spend long hours looking at the inn's collection of Fords. Each one is in mint running condition, the brass and chrome work gleam, and the upholstery is crisp and clean. Leo Powell, who is responsible for finding and rebuilding these machines, is usually around and proud to show you his work. A trip to the inn is a must for anyone seriously interested in antique automobiles.

After the autos, an exploratory trip into San Juan Capistrano is another must, if you can squeeze in the time. The place to see in Capistrano is the old San Juan Capistrano Mission, reputedly the oldest building in California and certainly the most senior and memorable of the whole remarkable chain of early missions that stretches up the coast—one every thirty miles, or a day's march from the next. Of course, this is the mission made famous by the Capistrano swallows, which return each year on March 19 from their winter haunts in South America. The mission covers an entire city block and is filled with historic inscriptions and archaeological artifacts, so allow two or three hours to cover it thoroughly.

Dining

The day begins at the Capistrano Inn with a delightful continental breakfast served on the terrace court or in your room, as you wish. Fresh orange juice and piping hot coffee accompany flaky croissants

San Juan Capistrano Mission, the oldest in California

and an ample supply of imported marmalade, more than enough fuel to get the day off to a good start.

Beyond this, food service at the inn is limited to a small garden terrace café that was recently opened to serve informal French country dishes, including quiches, omelets, salads, and sandwiches, from about 11 A.M. through the dinner hour.

Most people go out on the town for dinner, but first you have to decide which town. San Clemente, San Juan Capistrano, Dana Point, and Laguna Beach are all nearby, and the inn has menus of a representative group of good restaurants that will help point you in the right direction.

Olemendi's is the closest restaurant, just a couple of blocks north. It is unpretentious, both inside and out, but for those who like good Mexican food, it has a lot to offer. The walls are covered with autographed pictures of many luminaries who have expressed appreciation for the fine food. A few miles farther north, out on the wharf at Dana Point, are numerous restaurants of every variety. Casa Maria is another Mexican restaurant, but with an entirely different atmosphere. It is large, gaily decorated, and a gathering place where local residents and visitors can enjoy live mariachi music, margaritas, and dark Mexican beer along with their food. It is a jumping joint, with wall-to-wall people of all ages eating, drinking, talking, and singing.

Other recommended restaurants at Dana Point include the Quiet Cannon (which has excellent food, but is slowly slipping off a cliff, so no telling how long it will last), the Chart House, which serves especially fine food but charges accordingly, and Harpoon Henry's, an intriguingly named place on the end of the wharf with an excellent view of the boats moored along the dock.

The two best restaurants in San Juan Capistrano are in historic buildings. One of these is the unique Capistrano Depot in the restored 1895 Sante Fe train station. The building now serves as the Amtrak station, so you can watch the trains come and go while you dine. The other is the nearby El Adobe Restaurant, in a stagecoach station built in 1778. It serves old-time Californian and continental cuisine for lunch and dinner, and is well known for its Sunday brunches.

Rainbow Canyon Golf Resort

Distances:
   From San Diego—53 miles; allow 1 hour
   From Los Angeles—85 miles; allow 1½ hours
Features:
   A small, moderately priced resort devoted exclusively to golf, with
      generally agreeable weather year-round
Activities:
   Eighteen holes of golf, two tennis courts, pool, hot spa; located in
      one of California's premier horse-raising areas
Seasons:
   Open year-round; mid-January through April are the busiest
      months, May and June are slowest; July and August are
      popular with San Diegans and people from the desert;
      September, October, and November are often the prettiest
      time of year
Rates:
   $44 to $52 for two people weekdays; $48 to $54 weekends
Address:
   Box 129, Temecula, California 92390
Phone:
   (619) 676-5631

Rainbow Canyon Golf Resort

The special attractions of the Rainbow Canyon Golf Resort are the course, the weather, and the reasonably priced accommodations. The course, nestled into a lovely, tranquil valley, is management's pride and joy. The maintenance is meticulous and the overall quality is such that it is frequently chosen to host major tournaments and is on the Southern California Golf Association's list of official sites for qualifying rounds for the U.S. Open. There is no doubt that this is golf country. At the lodge they like to tell the story of one couple who come here frequently saying that they had actually counted sixty-eight other courses on the way from San Diego to Temecula to play Rainbow Canyon. The course is open to the public, but guests of the resort get preferential starting times (which they usually set at the same time as they make their room reservations).

Since this area is inland from the coast and separated from the desert by the Santa Rosa Mountains, the weather tends to be moderate year-round, so that people come from the north to escape the cold in winter, from the desert to escape the heat in summer, and from the coast to escape the heavier coastal fogs in the spring and fall. The accommodations are roomy, comfortable, and not overpriced, and the restaurant at the clubhouse has reliably good food and a friendly bar.

Rainbow Canyon used to be known as Rancho California Golf

Resort, but has changed its name to keep from being confused with a real estate development in the area. The resort's policy is to remain very low-key, and it does not advertise, but word of its high quality passing from golfer to golfer seems sufficient to maintain its popularity. This, in fact, is the subject of some mirth because people who have just "discovered" Rainbow Canyon all swear they will never tell anyone else in order to preserve their secret. But "everyone knows that golfers have big mouths" and are quite unable to resist telling friends about this find. So, possibly the word spreads faster when it's kept under wraps, in which case, who needs to advertise?

Routes and Distances

The town of Temecula and the area known as Rancho California appear to overlap on the map, causing some confusion. The Rainbow Canyon Golf Resort was once part of Rancho California but is no longer, and to clear up the confusion changed to its present name and took a Temecula address.

To get to the resort from the south, drive twenty-six miles past Escondido on Interstate 15 to the Temecula/Highway 79 exit. The golf course is plainly visible from the freeway. Take the exit and go east on 79 for a half-mile to Pala Road. There, go right less than a quarter-mile to the Rainbow Canyon Road and follow it to the resort.

From the north, the exit is marked Indio/Highway 79. At the end of the exit go left on 79, under the freeway, to Pala Road and Rainbow Canyon Road, as above.

Accommodations

Five modern, two-story frame buildings bordering the golf course house the eighty-five units at Rainbow Canyon. They are usually filled on weekends and holidays, but traffic is less heavy and reservations easier to get during the week. The accommodations are conveniently located in a pleasant setting, with prices we consider to be very reasonable for what is offered.

The top-of-the-line rooms are referred to on the rate sheet as the V.I.P. units. These are all corner rooms with window walls on two sides and sliding doors leading outside to either a deck or a patio. This feature expands the vista over the rolling hills of the golf course, giving the quarters an expansive, airy feeling. These rooms are large and are furnished with two double beds, a game table with four upholstered chairs, and a wet bar and refrigerator. There is also a roomy dressing room off of the bath.

The standard rooms are somewhat smaller, and do not have the wet bar, refrigerator, or separate dressing room, but they are more spacious than the average hotel room and are more than adequate for golfers who are out on the course most of the day.

The one other kind of accommodation, called a hospitality room, is especially useful for golfers traveling in a group. It consists of a large central room equipped with a wet bar and couches, with four standard bedrooms opening off of it. The central area is convenient for group activities and socializing, and no one has to go far when it's time to turn in.

Activities

Golf is undisputed king at Rainbow Canyon. Its 6789-yard, par-seventy-two course is one that pros from other clubs like to play, which helps explain why it is so often chosen as the site for tournaments. The front nine, on the valley floor, is relatively flat, but the back nine is hillier, and is dotted with picturesque oaks and rocky outcroppings. The thirteenth hole is particularly notorious for requiring precise ball placements to make the par of four. Since there are so many courses in the area, lodge guests who want variety and additional challenges will have no difficulty setting up starting times at other courses.

This resort does not stress tennis and has just two courts, located across the street from the lodge buildings, which seem to have been built as a sort of afterthought. They are nevertheless not a bad deal for tennis players, since there is no charge and seldom any trouble

Nearby Temecula is remodeled to replicate a frontier village

A day on the links at Rainbow Canyon

getting on. After tennis or golf, you can unwind in the pretty, heated swimming pool and hot whirlpool spa, located in a courtyard convenient to all the lodge buildings.

It is also worthwhile to find a little time to see some of the surrounding countryside in this rather unusual area. Rancho California and Temecula are horse-breeding country, where it is possible to see many beautiful animals grazing behind white board fences on equally beautiful estates along the back roads all around the resort.

Another attraction not to miss is the Wild Animal Park in Escondido. In this adjunct to the famous San Diego Zoo, you can observe from an open-sided train that travels around the park, zebras, giraffes, ostriches, and many other animals, all uncaged and occupying as nearly natural habitats as possible.

The town of Temecula, a mile from the resort, is becoming more interesting every year as its citizens and merchants proceed with an ambitious program to remodel it into a replica of a frontier village. A brand-new Frontier Museum and Historial Center is part of this effort, although, incongruously, it occupies a modern building in an industrial park just outside of town proper. It contains 25,000 square feet of displays and exhibits of the Old West, with stagecoaches, authentic weapons, and recreated scenes of famous gunfights and encampments—all worth a visit while you are so close at Rainbow Canyon.

Dining

The Rainbow Canyon Clubhouse is a large two-story building on the edge of the golf course. The upper level is occupied by two dining areas and a golfer's bar, the Tee Room. The main dining room overlooking the fairways and the hills beyond is the Rainbow Room, where you will ordinarily be served. If you are part of a large group you will be seated instead in the adjoining Terrace Room.

The three meals a day served in the Rainbow Room reflect the management philosophy that it is a mistake to try to get too fancy in a limited facility. It is better, they maintain, to keep the menu simple and make sure everything on it is good. We approve, and think they have been successful in this endeavor. Breakfast and lunch are standard fare, but tasty and well prepared. The dinner menu offers a variety of steaks, seafood, veal, and chicken, also well prepared and moderately priced.

The atmosphere in the Rainbow Room is pleasant, with a view over the golf course by day and an elaborately lit water fountain at night.

On the lower level, next to the pro shop, is a handy snack bar for golfers who want a quick bite before starting out or between nines. Coffee, juice, and sweet rolls are served in the morning, and an array of sandwiches, cold drinks, ice cream, and candy bars at lunchtime.

If you do not want to have dinner at the resort, the Packing House in the little town of nearby Fallbrook is reputed to be excellent. If you are willing to drive the twenty-six miles to Escondido, there are a number of good restaurants there, details about which are available in the resort office.

South Coastal
Getaways

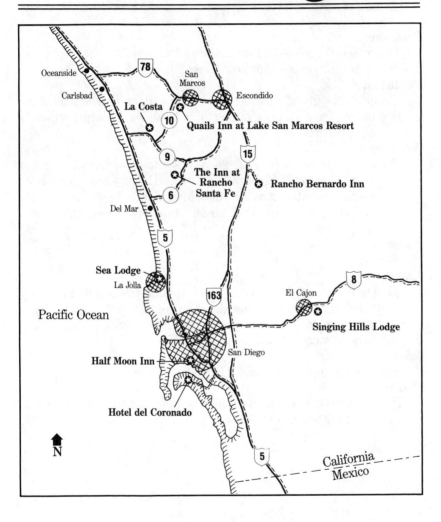

Oceanside

Carlsbad

78

San Marcos

Escondido

La Costa

10

Quails Inn at Lake San Marcos Resort

9

15

The Inn at Rancho Santa Fe

6

Rancho Bernardo Inn

Del Mar

5

Sea Lodge

La Jolla

163

8

El Cajon

Pacific Ocean

Singing Hills Lodge

Half Moon Inn

San Diego

Hotel del Coronado

N

5

California

Mexico

La Costa

Distances:
From San Diego—30 miles; allow 45 minutes
From Los Angeles—85 miles; allow 2 hours

Features:
Generally delightful weather and a wide variety of diversions draw people from all over the country to this very large, superbly equipped resort

Activities:
Twenty-seven holes of golf, 25 tennis courts, 4 heated outdoor swimming pools, elaborate health and beauty spas, horseback riding, nightly movies, dancing, duplicate bridge, backgammon, volleyball, and miscellaneous events organized on a daily basis

Seasons:
Year-round

Rates:
$110 to $135 for two people; suites and villas from $165; Spa Plan, which includes room, meals, spa program, golf, and tennis is $365 per day for two, plus 15 percent service charge and 6 percent tax, with a four-day minimum

Address:
Rancho La Costa, Carlsbad, California 92008

Phone:
(619) 438-9111; toll free in California (800) 542-6200; toll free outside California (800) 854-6564

Château units are close to the racquet club

La Costa has a reputation as a place people come back to, and a surprising number make it a practice to do this regularly, not just once but three or four times a year. They come because they like the weather and for the programs—especially the spa program, which many have come to depend upon for keeping in shape. Of the eight hundred or nine hundred guests that may be here at any one time, a third or more are usually on the spa program.

First-timers will be impressed at the amount of activity around the main hotel entrance and lobby: the number of limousines coming and going, tennis players hurrying to the courts with rackets in hand, golfers driving by in their carts, and men and women in warm-up suits walking briskly to their appointments at the spa.

Despite the number of limousines out front, La Costa is not just a hangout for celebrities. Many celebrities do come here, but most of them come precisely because they can get lost in the crowd and enjoy the same relaxation and healthy renewal as everyone else. The surprise of La Costa is that there is nothing stuffy about it. People smile and say "hello" to complete strangers, and in such an atmosphere it takes little time to get caught up in the spirit and plunge right into all the things there are to do.

La Costa is not cheap, but guests get their money's worth, and there are many places with less to offer that charge more. This is a major tennis resort, a major golf resort, and a preeminent health spa all rolled into one, under an umbrella of nearly ideal weather.

Routes and Distances

From either north or south on Interstate 5, about ten miles south of Oceanside and thirty miles north of downtown San Diego, look for the La Costa Avenue exit. Go east on La Costa Avenue, following a tidal inlet for about a mile to El Camino Real. Go left a very short distance on El Camino Real, past a small shopping mall, to the unmistakable La Costa resort entrance.

Accommodations

Six completely separate and different kinds of accommodations are available, so you should consider carefully to decide which will suit you best.

If you are on the Spa Plan, you will usually be assigned to and will want to be in one of the spa rooms, as these are all grouped together around their own outdoor pool, next to the spa itself. These rooms are really miniature suites, with sitting areas and separate dressing rooms. If rented separately, they would be more expensive than the main building rooms, but for those on the plan the room cost is included in the total package.

The main building, also referred to as "the hotel," houses 130 rooms

Health-spa guests have a private pool

and is connected directly to the clubhouse, where the restaurants and many of the recreational facilities are located. The hotel has the most convenient and least expensive quarters. Its rooms are all large and comfortable, with two queen beds and sumptuous baths.

Next on the list are seven golf cottages—separate buildings arranged in a row facing one of the fairways—and two tennis cottages near the racquet club. Each of these cottages contains five modern, spick-and-span, hotel-type rooms, each with its own little patio or deck and outdoor furniture. These rooms are the same price as those in the main building.

Priced about twenty percent higher are a large block of château accommodations in two buildings close to the tennis courts, each with its own private swimming pool. The châteaus are particularly comfortable since they are privately owned condominiums, for rent during the fifty weeks of the year their owners are not using them. They consist of living room–bedroom combinations with wet bars and an unusual arrangement whereby two electrically operated queen beds come out of the wall for sleeping.

Two kinds of complete houses are also available for families and groups traveling together. The La Costa villas are the smallest, with two or three bedrooms, two baths, living room, dining room, and complete kitchen, all very nicely furnished and comfortable, especially for extended stays. Finally, there are six large, luxurious, expensive executive homes, each one very elegantly decorated and furnished, with a private garage, a yard, and several patios arranged so the occupants can catch the sun at any time of the day.

Activities

The La Costa Health Spa, which has been in operation for nearly twenty years, is an acknowledged leader in what is becoming an increasingly popular way for people to maintain their personal appearance and health. The physical plant consists of two identical facilities set side by side, one for men and one for women. The buildings are attractively furnished and decorated in colors intended to induce relaxation. They are also filled with exercise and therapy equipment, some of it very unusual, and a full staff of professional attendants trained to understand and accommodate each patron's particular needs.

When you enter the spa building at your appointed time, you get a locker and exchange your regular clothes for a sort of brief terry cloth toga and a pair of sandals. You move from activity to activity in groups, which facilitates making acquaintances.

The minimum program lasts for four days, during which participants are encouraged to concentrate intensively on themselves, not only for physical rejuvenation and mental stimulation, but also, it is hoped, to achieve a sort of spiritual renewal. The spa attempts to send participants home slimmer, healthier, and with an improved self-image. The program is strenuous, with days consisting of brisk walks, fitness classes, water exercises, yoga, diet control lectures, and calorie-controlled meals. There is a lot of physical exertion, but it is rewarded with long, luxurious body massages performed outside under sunny skies in a walled courtyard by a pool, followed by relaxing facials, milkbaths, herbal wraps, Swiss showers, and intensive skin care instruction. Time is allowed for long soaks in an array of varied temperature Roman baths in a glass-enclosed atrium, where people can also stretch out in the sunshine to read or explore their private thoughts at leisure.

Despite the busy schedule, spa guests have some time to participate in the many other activities available at La Costa, just as regular guests can take advantage of specific spa treatments, such as massages and facials, by special appointment. Among these regular activities, the tennis program is probably the best known because it is headed by the well-liked Pancho Segura, acknowledged as one of the country's half-dozen best teaching professionals. The tennis complex has twenty-five courts, and there are always a lot of people about, playing, watching, or looking for games. A skilled tennis hostess helps match players to make games, which is helpful to newcomers who are eager to play but don't know anyone. A large grandstand area en-

Center court at La Costa Tennis Club

circling a central court provides a perfect setup for the several major tournaments hosted here each year, the best known of which is the Carl Reiner Pro-Celebrity held each June.

The twenty-seven-hole championship golf course is also the scene of several major tournaments, including the annual Tournament of Champions. This course is kept in top condition and, because it is so big, it is seldom overcrowded. It is a pro's favorite, but still not overly intimidating to country club players, except perhaps for a few holes like the 565-yard seventeenth, known affectionately as "the monster," which has traps all along the left side of the fairway and water on the right. An excellent professional staff and well-equipped pro shop are, of course, part of the golf facilities. Greens fees are $25, and use of the tennis courts is charged at $10 per hour for two, $12 for four; there is no charge in either case for Spa Plan guests.

Horseback riders can arrange trail rides into the surrounding foothills by calling the stables, located to the south of the tennis courts, for a reservation on one of the several rides that go out daily Tuesday through Sunday. After pursuing some of these active sports, a swim and a sunbath at one of the four pools scattered on the grounds can be refreshing. The main pool at the clubhouse is Olympic size, and attractive to serious swimmers who want to do laps.

La Costa is not one of those resorts where things wind down at night. Dancing in the Continental Room goes on long after the dinner hour, and a group in the lounge provides live music for listening and dancing. Often, guests receive dancing lessons here to get them started on the new, popular steps.

There is a backgammon room on the upper level of the clubhouse, with games going on nightly. Everyone is welcome and lessons are available. The cardroom downstairs, for bridge and canasta, is also generally busy in the evening. At one end of the clubhouse is the resort's own theater, which shows good recent movies every night for only $1.50.

The staff also arranges for a variety of special events daily, including junkets to the San Diego Zoo, Sea World, bullfights in Tijuana, the racetrack at Del Mar, shops in La Jolla, and to the ocean beaches for a day of sun and swimming. Additionally, there are bingo parties, duplicate bridge tournaments where ACES master points are awarded, and occasional bridge lectures.

It is a busy schedule, and to keep guests informed about what is going on, a program listing each day's events is on guests' tables each morning at breakfast.

Dining

It is unusual, even in a resort as large as La Costa, to find four first-class restaurants, each with its own special cuisine.

The Continental Dining Room on the main level of the clubhouse is the central hub of activity and a contrast to the other three. Where they are small and intimate, the Continental is a cavernous room, filled with bustle and activity all day. It is the only one of the four that serves breakfast and lunch as well as dinner, but when the dinner hour comes, it undergoes such a complete change of character that even the name is changed. It then becomes the Continental After Dark and, with the addition of fine linen, gleaming silver, and candlelight, it takes on the elegant ambience of the other dining rooms. Strolling violinists serenade the diners, and later a trio comes on to provide music for dinner dancing. The atmosphere here has a certain formality in the evening, and gentlemen are requested to wear jackets to dinner. On Sundays a hunt breakfast is served in the Continental Room from 7:00 A.M. until 2:30 P.M., followed by a Sunday buffet, which is a special event at La Costa.

The second and third dinner houses are downstairs in the clubhouse. Both are delightful, informal, and have entirely different menus. The Steak House features an array of steaks, all cooked to perfection over charcoal, as well as prime rib and chops. The salad bar here is unusually good, with such delicacies as shrimp, artichoke hearts, and avocado, and the thinly sliced, over-crisped pumpernickel bread with Parmesan cheese is hard to resist. The Steak House is rather small and always busy, so reservations are necessary.

The Seville Room, downstairs across from The Steak House, is also small and intimate and specializes in Italian food. All kinds of veal dishes, scampi, seafood, and pasta are served here, and they are all very good. This room, too, is informal, but things are done with a flourish by a corps of deft waiters who concoct the salads and entrées right at tableside.

The fourth restaurant is La Costa's elegant, expensive Pisces, located a couple of blocks outside the entrance gate at the La Costa Plaza. The atmosphere is also formal at Pisces, and gentlemen must wear jackets. The menu is an elaborate array of seafood specialties, including Maine and imported lobster and many exotic dishes, all highly recommended.

One more place to eat, which many count on to suffice for lunch, is a small snack bar in the second floor of the Racquet Club. The open deck that looks directly down to the championship court, where some action is usually under way, is a pleasant place for a beer and a sandwich.

Quails Inn at Lake San Marcos Resort

Distances:
> From downtown Los Angeles—97 miles; allow 2 hours
> From San Diego—30 miles; allow 45 minutes

Features:
> A medium-sized resort boasting 340 sunny, smog-free days a year is located on quiet, pretty little Lake San Marcos; no organized activities to pressure you; just do what you want when you want

Activities:
> Two golf courses, tennis, paddle ball, two swimming pools, lake boating

Seasons:
> Year-round

Rates:
> $40 to $50 for two people weekdays, $45 to $55 weekends; one-bedroom and two-bedroom apartments with kitchenettes $65 to $110

Address:
> 1025 La Bonita Drive, Lake San Marcos, California 92069

Phone:
> (619) 744-0120

Quails Inn on Lake San Marcos

Consistently good weather is the raison d'être for this unusual resort. Lake San Marcos is located at one corner of a relatively small miniclime known at "the La Jolla triangle," where the average temperature varies no more than twenty degrees year-round, a phenomenon known to exist in only two other places—the French Riviera and a part of New Zealand. It is truly the "world's most perfect climate" and draws people to its comforts from the big cities' summer heat.

The lake is partly responsible for the moderate temperatures, but more important are gentle breezes that come down the narrow canyons carrying cool ocean air inland in the summer and warmer desert air the other way in winter. Ninety-degree temperatures are common in Escondido in the summer but nearly unheard of at Lake San Marcos, although the two are only a few miles apart.

January is the rainy month here, but for the most part winters are more like summer farther north—perfect for golf and tennis—and that brings down the "snowbirds," as the natives call them, who come from Seattle, Minneapolis, and points east to get away from winter and onto the links and the courts.

Lake San Marcos is a man-made lake around which a controlled development was designed, with the resort at one end. This part of the lake is rimmed by attractive houses, but the upper half of the lake, ending at a concrete dam that spans the canyon, is still bordered by same empty, sage-covered hills that have been there for thousands of years.

Surrey-topped, motor-driven barges called "kayots" are standard transportation on the lake. Every house has its kayot tied up in front, and the inn, in keeping with the custom, has some of its own for rent to guests. Many lake residents have their evening libations afloat, so in the late afternoons there are often processions of the gaily colored craft, with their occupants waving and exchanging pleasantries as they pass.

Quails Inn is not as isolated as some of the other resorts included here—a small shopping mall is right across the street, for example—but it has all the accoutrements of an attractive getaway: restaurants and lounges, tennis, golf, and swimming, generally fine weather, and reasonable prices.

Routes and Distances

From San Diego, drive north on Interstate 15 to Escondido and turn west on California 78 to San Marcos. At San Marcos, go left on San Marcos Boulevard a short distance to Rancho Santa Fe Road. Go left again there for a quarter-mile to the Lake San Marcos and Quails Inn sign on the left.

From the north, come down Interstate 5 to Oceanside go east on California 78. Watch for exit signs to Lake San Marcos and the Rancho Santa Fe Road. Take the Rancho Santa Fe Road approximately two miles to the Lake San Marcos and Quails Inn sign.

Accommodations

Quails Inn is relatively new and has eighty rental units. All its rooms are in one- and two-story buildings set slightly back from the lake to allow room for two swimming pools and a lakefront drive. The four kinds of rooms, in order of our preference, are deluxe lake view, pool view, deluxe, and standard. The price difference between the cheapest and most expensive is only ten dollars, so you might as well opt for the premium rooms if you can. The differences in price are determined strictly by the size and location of the rooms, which are all attractive, light, and clean.

The lake view rooms, in the newest building, are good, big rooms, which have separate dressing areas and plenty of space for king or twin beds, a large closet, a vanity, table and chairs, cable television, and a furnished deck or patio area. The deluxe rooms on the opposite side of this building are exactly the same, but instead of looking at the lake face inland toward the shopping mall.

The rooms in the other buildings are just a bit smaller, without space for the extra table and chairs in the bedroom, but are otherwise very similar. Half of these overlook the pools and the others, facing inland, are the standard rooms.

The advantage of the pool view rooms, especially those on the first floor, is that they open directly onto the two swimming pools, which are no more than twenty feet from the entrance doors. All rooms are five dollars more on weekends.

In addition, there are four very appealing lakeshore apartments, but they are often reserved well in advance. They offer a great deal of privacy and are right on the water's edge. Each has its own kitchenette, making them particularly useful for family groups.

Activities

Lake San Marcos is the focal point for guests of the inn, who can begin their explorations by renting one of the kayots to explore the waterfront. These flattopped craft, built on pontoons and powered by a light outboard, seat up to eight people without crowding. Although they proceed at stately speed, they can still make it all the way to the end of the lake and back in an hour. You can begin by circling the lower lakeshore, looking at all the pretty waterfront homes and the waterfowl swimming around their island nesting grounds and enjoying the cool lake breezes, then proceed down to the unpopulated end of the lake to see the citrus groves, barren hills, and finally the high dam that has formed the lake.

The boat rental dock is located just beyond the restaurant

"Kayots" or slow boats for rent on Lake San Marcos

building. In addition to kayots, it has canoes, rowboats, small sail-boats, and aqua bikes all lined up ready to take out.

Lake San Marcos is not suitable for swimming, but inn guests have their choice of two nearly identical pools side by side—one kept warm and the other cool.

The inn maintains use privileges for its guests at two local golf courses. The private Lake San Marcos Country Club is within easy walking distance of the inn and has a challenging 6500-yard, eighteen-hole championship course, complete with pro shop, food and bar serv-ices, and all the other usual amenities. Less ambitious or less accom-plished golfers might prefer the public par-fifty-eight Lakeview ex-ecutive course about a half-mile in the other direction from the inn. Lakeview is a sporty eighteen holes on rolling terrain, and with greens fees of only $5.50 it affords golfers an opportunity to practice their short game at very low cost.

The Racquet Club, only a few hundred feet past the restaurant buildings, has four beautifully maintained, individually fenced regula-tion tennis courts and three paddle ball courts—the latter is a very popular sport in these parts. Use of the Racquet Club is free to inn guests, and paddle ball equipment is available at the front desk.

Dining

Quails Inn Dinner House is built on the very edge of Lake San Marcos, with the bar on the lower level and the dining room above both cantilevered right out over the water—an impressive setting for leisurely lunches and dinners.

This is a large restaurant, seating 450 when all its tables are filled—which is many more people than can possibly stay at the inn. It usually is full, too, and bustling with activitiy, a sign of its popularity with local residents as well as inn guests.

A variety of special features all week long contribute to this popularity. One of them is a daily prime rib luncheon buffet that in-cludes a seafood salad bar and provides hearty eating at a quite reasonable price. Another is the special Polynesian luau buffet on Monday nights. Monday is usually a slack time in the restaurant business, but not here. All diners receive gaily colored leis when they come in, and then are treated to an array of roast pork, sweet and sour barbecued spareribs, teriyaki chicken, sweet potatoes, a variety of seafood, and salad and dessert selections.

Sunday evenings feature another prime rib buffet, and during the rest of the week you can choose from a menu with thirty-two entrées. All these dinners, like the luncheons, are surprisingly reasonably priced, which is one of the reasons the Dinner House is always full.

The alternative to the Dinner House is the China House Res-

Coffee and a Danish in the morning sun

taurant at the country club. It is small and cozy and serves very good
Chinese and American food. Both the China House and its adjoining
bar look out over the golf course, so you can sit in comfort and watch
the agony and the ecstasy outside as the golfers come and go.

Neither of these two restaurants is open for breakfast, but you
can go across the street to the shopping mall, where an excellent little
Danish bakery serves juices, pastries, and coffee you can enjoy in the
morning sun at a sidewalk table.

The Inn at Rancho Santa Fe

Distances:

From San Diego—25 miles; allow ½ hour

From Los Angeles—107 miles: allow 2¼ hours

Features:

One of California's oldest, loveliest inns, in an exceptionally beautiful area close to San Diego; moderate weather year-round attracts easterners in the winter and southern Californians in summer

Activities:

Tennis, swimming in heated pool, lawn croquet; three golf courses nearby; use of cottage on the ocean at Del Mar beach

Seasons:

Year-round; "winter" here is February through Easter; July through Labor Day is the busiest period; October, November, and December are slow, but are often the prettiest months

Rates:

Great variety of room sizes and locations, and correspondingly wide range of rates: $40 to $150 per night for two people, with the average about $65 to $70

Address:

P.O. Box 869, Rancho Santa Fe, California 92067

Phone:

(619) 756-1131

Built in 1923, the inn reflects the California mission style

The little community of Rancho Santa Fe has a most unusual history. It takes its name from the Santa Fe Railroad, which bought eight thousand acres of Mexican land grant property in 1906 with the intention of propagating fast-growing eucalyptus trees for railroad ties. Over three million seedlings from Australia were planted, and the trees thrived; unfortunately, the wood proved useless for ties and the railroad was stuck with the property. But there was a silver lining. If eucalyptus would grow, so might citrus, so the undaunted railroad set aside all the remaining land for orchards, while the part now beautifully shaded by eucalyptus was to become a residential development.

Today, Rancho Santa Fe is one of the oldest and loveliest planned communities in California. The inn, occupying twenty-one of the most desirable acres, was built in 1923 to accommodate prospective land buyers. A rambling building of adobe bricks made from local mud and straw, it became a model for the California mission style of architecture that others in the area imitated and that has been faithfully followed since, giving the village a remarkable homogeneity. Since the neighboring properties are a minimum size of one acre and most of the homes are surrounded by citrus groves and pasture, the area has a rural atmosphere.

For three generations, a family named Royce has owned and personally managed the inn, fostering in the process a strong sense of continuity and tradition. The entrance lounge, for instance, which is a large thirty-by-forty-foot room with a lovely cathedral ceiling, is more like the living room of the family home, and is appropriately filled with treasures and antiques collected by the Royces from all over Europe and Asia. They include a priceless collection of wooden ship models, some over 150 years old, mounted high on the walls, while below are interesting Japanese prints and screens, and ornate, hand-carved antique furniture, always accented with bouquets of fresh flowers from the inn's own gardens. Outside, the main inn building is surrounded by sweeping green lawns and flower beds, and cottages hidden by shrubbery.

This, in short, is a lovely and gracious place to stay, and it offers the additional advantage of the La Jolla Triangle's unique weather pattern, where annual temperatures usually fall between sixty-five and eighty degrees. The reason, we were told, is that when the land heats up in the summer the hot air rises and draws cooler ocean air inland through the canyons, while in winter, warm Santa Ana winds from the desert flow the other way and gently warm the triangle.

In any event, the weather is remarkably stable, smog-free, and suited to outdoor activities, and that is reason enough for city folk to make this trip and see it for themselves.

Routes and Distances

Look for Rancho Santa Fe on your road map only twenty-five miles north of San Diego between Solana Beach and Escondido, about five miles east of U.S. 101 on County Road S6. The county road connects the coast to Escondido and goes directly through Rancho Santa Fe. The inn is at the south end of the village, well marked and easy to recognize.

Accommodations

It is difficult to photograph the cottages because of the way they are scattered on the property and tucked in among the trees and plantings. It is nearly as difficult to describe them, because they come in such a variety of shapes and sizes and locations.

About a quarter of the accommodations are in the main inn building; all the rest are in one of the twenty cottages. If your room is in one of the latter, you will need a map of the grounds to find your way the first time.

The rooms on the low end of the price scale are the smallest and are all located in the inn building. They are also the oldest and, although they do not have a sitting area or private patio, they contain pleasant white furniture and bright decor and are close to the restaurants and swimming pool and other centers of attraction, mak-

Cottages for rent, surrounded by eucalyptus trees

ing them most livable and popular. There are also a few larger rooms in the main building, and even some two-room suites. Next, overlooking the croquet lawn directly across from the inn is a long, low structure containing another group of four attractively furnished units, each of which has a spacious sitting room adjacent to the bedroom.

After that comes a number of medium-sized, medium-priced cottage units, best described as large bed–sitting room combinations, with the additional advantage of private patios or sun decks.

At the upper end of the price range, there are many large cottage units, which all include separate sitting rooms, outdoor patios, and a variety of extra amenities such as fireplaces or kitchenettes or wet bars.

All the rooms have air conditioning, television, and telephones, and all but the smallest also have a half-size refrigerator. The beds are all two twins, which can be converted to a king on request.

Those who travel with pets will be pleased to learn that a dog is welcome to stay with its family in certain units. There is a charge of ten dollars for housing a pet, and the inn is careful to point out that the American Plan does not apply, so owners must bring their animals' own food supplies.

Activities
The inn has three of the better tennis courts we have seen in the

past year, each one individually fenced and screened and set in a eucalyptus grove for additional wind protection. These are exclusively for the use of inn guests, at no charge, on a first-come, first-served basis. The courts are kept locked; you pick up the key at the front desk whenever you want to play.

If golf is your preference, there are three courses in the vicinity where the inn can make arrangements for its guests to play. The closest course is the Rancho Santa Fe Country Club, just a quarter-mile distant which, however, is available to inn guests only after noon; mornings are reserved for members only. It is considered a challenging course and charges $27.50 greens fees. Whispering Palms, two miles distant and half as expensive, is a relatively flat public course where it is hard to lose your ball. The Lomas executive golf course, also about two miles away, in a well-groomed, hilly setting, suits some people better than the big courses. It has a full eighteen holes, but all are short, par-three.

On the lawn in front of the inn is a magnificent croquet course, maintained and played in the traditional manner. Gentlemen players wear white slacks and shirts; ladies wear white skirts, and a game under way is always a colorful event that draws galleries along the surrounding walkways.

In the summertime it is only a twelve-minute drive seven miles to the beach cottage at Del Mar, which is maintained for exclusive use of inn guests. We consider the Del Mar beach to be one of the nicest and safest in all Southern California. It is wide and smooth, with a very shallow gradient, so the water is pleasant for swimming and free from undertow; yet the rollers that come in are often fine for surfing, which is popular here and entertaining to watch. The beach house has bath and dressing facilities, a comfortable living room, a kitchen, outdoor barbecues, and a wind-screened deck. As with the tennis courts, you will be given an entrance key at the front desk, and there is no charge. A beachboy is in attendance in summer to supply towels and beach chairs and other necessities. This is great beach for early morning joggers and beach walkers. The gold-flecked sand, colored by specks of iron pyrite (fool's gold), is an unusual and arresting sight.

From July to September, the big activity in these parts is the Del Mar thoroughbred racing season, and the inn invariably fills to capacity with aficionados. The track is on the way to the beach house, only minutes from the inn, so it is easy to visit both on the same afternoon.

Despite the number of "active" activities available, the management tells us half their guests don't come to do anything but relax. They may stroll about the grounds to look at the flowers, or into the immaculate little village to see the shops and the expensive dwellings, or they may take books from the inn's two-thousand-volume library to

The inn has a beach house at nearby Del Mar

read by the swimming pool. A lot of them just lie in the sun. For whatever reasons, the history of the inn shows that half of the guests each season have been there at least once before.

Dining

There is no town square in the village of Rancho Santa Fe, but if there were, the inn and its broad lawn would be on the perfect site for it—right at the point where the two main streets come together and the small row of shops begins. It is an easy walk into town, and anyone who wants to eat out will find a choice of restaurants to try, all of them places with "personalities," which makes them fun to visit. The first one you come to, Mille Fleurs, serves French cooking in a little mall that has outdoor tables in warm weather. The Doorway and Quimby's, two more just down the street, are also worth looking into.

A number of other good places are a short drive outside of town, at Del Mar and Solana Beach along the coast.

But once people have eaten at the inn itself, it is hard to lure them away. Reasonable prices, attentive service, and generally first-class cooking are its pride and continuing commitment. The inn has two separate dining rooms, and when reservations are in order during busy seasons, you must make yours in one or the other. The menus are the same in both rooms, however, which are serviced by a common kitchen. The Garden Room, overlooking the swimming pool, serves all three meals every day and is the more formal of the two. The Vintage Room, which serves only lunch and dinner, is quite different. It actually is three rooms surrounding an enclosed patio, making a fourth area for outdoor dining—at lunchtime the patio is the favored place to eat. It is filled with live orchids and azaleas or poinsettias, depending on the season, and is always colorful, fragrant, and delightful for a leisurely meal. On warm summer evenings on Fridays and Saturdays, the tables are arranged around the perimeter to clear a floor in the center for dancing under the stars. Music is played by an old-time trio that has played here for years, doing familiar music that is easy to follow. Even people who haven't danced for a long time can find themselves getting back into the swing at these weekend events, which are now a well-established tradition.

During the day, informal or casual dress is the rule in the dining rooms. Men are expected to wear jackets after six, and women to dress more formally than they do in the daytime.

Rancho Bernardo Inn

Distances:

From downtown San Diego—20 miles; allow ½ hour

From Los Angeles—112 miles; allow 2½ hours

Features:

One of Southern California's larger golf and tennis resorts; recent extensive renovations have made it elegant in every respect; not inexpensive, but visitors can take advantage of package plans that offer savings

Activities:

Golf, tennis, tennis college instruction, swimming, Jacuzzis, gourmet dining, sight-seeing in San Diego and Mexico

Season:

Year-round

Rates:

January through mid-April, $105 to $130 for two people; mid-April through June, $85 to $115; July to mid-September, $75 to $105; mid-September through December, $85 to $115; suites available; four-day, three-night "holiday packages," including breakfast, dinner, and all playing fees are $266 per person

Address:

17550 Bernardo Oaks Drive, San Diego, California 92128

Phone:

(619) 487-1611; toll free in California (800) 542-6096; toll free outside California (800) 854-1065

Checking in at Rancho Bernardo Inn

You can usually expect fine, sunny weather at Rancho Bernardo, although once in a while in the spring a bit of coastal fog will sneak up the valleys and blanket the countryside—not enough, however, to disrupt the tennis and golf that are two of the three main attractions here. The third is the fine dining.

Unlike most resorts, which offer special rates and packages off-season and midweek to fill in gaps in their bookings, the best bargains at Rancho Bernardo are the four-day, three-night tennis and golf "holiday" packages available any time of the year. Most of the inn's guests arrange their visits to take advantage of these packages.

It is possible, of course, to come at the regular room rates and pay individually for meals, greens fees, and court time. Modest eaters and those who expect to play infrequently will find this acceptable; but with the package, you can play as much and as long as you wish all four days and have anything you desire from either of the restaurants for breakfast and dinner during your stay. This is important if good food is high on your list of priorities, because the Rancho's El Bizcocho dinner restaurant is by every measure among the three or four finest in Southern California. And, as might be expected, it is not inexpensive. But when you come on the package, you can pamper yourself there every night and be quite unconcerned with the size of the bill.

Moreover, should you come in by air to the San Diego International Airport, the package includes transportation to and from the inn at no extra charge, a not inconsiderable item. The only things not covered are taxes, gratuities, alcoholic beverages, and luncheons; these you pay for in the usual manner.

Upon first arriving at the inn you will see that it is typical gracious California mission architecture, with low, tile-roofed buildings and wide overhanging eves. It will be obvious that no expense was spared during the big renovation program of a few years ago. Inside the lobby are several spacious lounge areas, studded with antiques and many genuine oriental rugs and art objects. The Music Room contains card tables, conversation nooks, and a grand piano. Complimentary tea, cookies, and sherry are served here every evening between four and five, and on Sunday mornings, before the brunch, free bowls of screwdrivers and bloody marys are set out to start the day. Across from the Music Room, the Fireside Room is similarly furnished, with a fire always blazing in the fireplace at one end and more deeply upholstered conversation groupings, plus a row of chess and checkers consoles.

Beyond the front desk, through French doors, is a wide garden court surrounded by guest rooms and containing two separate swimming pools and two Jacuzzi spas. Off the lobby to the left is the famous "El Biz" dinner house, while downstairs on the lower level is another restaurant, The Veranda Room, which opens onto a picturesque outdoor dining terrace. Overlooking the tennis facilities, the golf course's first tee, and the whole emerald valley below, it is understandably the favorite luncheon spot in this community.

Routes and Distances

The town of Rancho Bernardo lies just east of Interstate 15, approximately two-thirds of the way between San Diego and Escondido.

From Los Angeles, take I-5 to Oceanside, and California 78 from there to Escondido. At Escondido take I-15 south to the Rancho Bernardo exit.

From San Diego go north on Interstate 15 twenty miles from downtown to the Rancho Bernardo exit.

From either north or south, the exit places you on Rancho Bernardo Road, where you proceed east ¾-mile to Bernardo Oaks Drive. Turn left there for another mile. The drive terminates at the entrance to the inn.

Accommodations

Except for a few executive suites, used mainly by leaders of conference groups, all the rooms at Rancho Bernardo are regular hotel rooms, approximately the same size and quite similarly furnished. The

Mission-style rooms overlook the courtyard

range of prices among rooms is based on the view and type of bed. The most expensive rooms have a golf view, meaning they look out across the valley and a good portion of the golf course, and have one king bed. The king bed allows space in the room for a sitting area with a couch and coffee table, making it a kind of junior suite. All other rooms have two queen beds. Some of these, too, have a golf view, some face onto the swimming pool courtyards, a few look out toward the mountains, and a very few are situated with little or no view (and bear the lowest prices).

Every room has a private, furnished balcony or patio, and all are tastefully decorated with lined drapes, thick quilted bedspreads, and double sheeting on the beds. A typical room with two queen beds will also have a round card table and two upholstered armchairs, a lounge chair with a hassock and floor lamp for reading, a dresser, television set, and telephone. It will also have a small refrigerator in an alcove, a roomy closet, and two sinks in the bath area, one in a well-lighted vanity alcove and the other in the bathroom itself.

The 232 accommodations at the inn are actually located in seven separate buildings grouped around the main inn complex. People who come on one of the package plans are usually assigned rooms, if possible, in the buildings most appropriate to what they intend to do, with golfers in the building close to the first tee and tennis players near the tennis college. If you are on one of the packages, room price is no consideration, and you may well be assigned one of the most expensive rooms. For those paying the regular rates, not on a package, we think the midpriced poolside rooms in the 100, 200, and 300 buildings are the best bargains, mainly because they are the most conveniently located to all of the inn's facilities, and because the courtyards they face onto afford most pleasant views.

If you are coming to Rancho Bernardo with a group of people who all plan to participate in the same activity, every effort will be made to put you together. A golfing group, for example, would normally be lodged in the 700 building, housing the rooms closest to the first tee.

Activities

Rancho Bernardo has been known for over twenty years as a major center for both golf and tennis. The multimillion dollar expansion and renovation that was completed in the early 1980s has further enhanced its reputation. In 1980 over $500,000 was spent to reconstruct and rehabilitate the golf course in order to correct a silting problem that sometimes caused the course to flood in the spring. Now the eighteen-hole West Course is in top tournament condition and the fairways are kept emerald green year-round by a technique of over-seeding the bermuda turf with perennial rye. This par-seventy-two course is considered one of the more challenging on the West Coast because of the variety of hazards the golfer must circumvent. Four lakes, a number of ponds, several streams, and a couple of waterfalls constitute the water hazards and these, combined with sand traps, huge trees, and a precarious rough, exact a toll for any badly hit ball. The course is laid out on rolling hills, which enhances its tranquil beauty but can give golfers fits with tees that often are either uphill or downhill and take considerable talent to negotiate.

Perhaps less challenging, but tricky in its own way, is the Oaks North Executive Course at Rancho Bernardo. It is a twenty-seven-hole layout, with each of the three nines a par-thirty. Like the West Course, it is set amid beautiful natural surroundings.

The resort, of course, has a full service pro shop, with complete equipment and accessories and a staff of professionals on hand for group or private lessons.

Tennis receives as much careful attention here as golf does. The tennis facility is now considered one of the finest in the country, after also being upgraded and modernized during the renovation. The complex boasts twelve excellent courts (four lighted for night play), a viewing gallery, an excellent pro shop, and a full staff of professionals, all certified USPTA, who conduct the series of "intensive college" programs. Most tennis players come on one of the package pro-

The Rancho Bernardo is a center for golf

grams and then enroll in the college, which offers sessions of either two, four, or five days. The two-day clinics held weekly on Thursday and Friday and on Saturday and Sunday emphasize basic strokes. On Monday and Tuesday, the emphasis is put on strategy. Those wanting complete instruction in both strokes and strategy stay the four days, Saturday through Tuesday.

The five-day clinic is only held once a month, usually during the third week, and is a big event. It begins with a gala cocktail party on the first night, and is great fun, thanks to such fringe benefits as picture-taking, college tee shirts, and chances to meet and joke with the instructors. The teaching is dead serious, however, at all the clinics. Each day's instruction includes about five hours of lessons, with groups of five or six players moving to a series of stations where different instructors work on every aspect of the game. The college has four full-time professionals besides the head coach, Paul Navitril, who has directed the program for eight years. The enrollment of each clinic is limited to between twenty and twenty-five pupils.

Of course, not everyone enrolls in the tennis college, and most of the courts are open for casual play. Reservations are usually necessary, but there is no limit to use for those on the package plan. People on a straight rate should also make reservations in advance, and they will be charged a moderate fee. The staff will try to set up games, if at all possible, for those who want competition.

Two delightful swimming pools and three Jacuzzis are favorite spots with returning golfers and tennis players, as well as with those who simply enjoy lounging and relaxing. Other leisure activities at the inn include volleyball on the lawn, ping-pong, shuffleboard, and bicycles that can be rented from the bell captain, who will also arrange transportation and make reservations at a nearby stables for those wishing to ride horseback.

Dining

The Inn has two fine restaurants to entertain its guests and anyone staying a couple of days would be remiss not to experience them both. The Veranda, which serves three meals a day, has been recently redecorated and refurbished and is quite elegant, but still retains a casual atmosphere. Guests can be comfortable in golf or tennis togs at lunch or breakfast, and jackets are not required at the dinner hour. Its large terrace, covered with umbrella tables, is a fine place on sunny days to try the special cobb salad or one of its delicious sandwiches. Dinner is also a pleasant time in the Veranda for those on a package plan and, with the sky the limit, a lot of the crowd go for the boiled Maine lobster, a house specialty, or perhaps the beef Wellington.

The prize of Rancho Bernardo, however, is its famous El Bizcocho restaurant on the main level of the inn. When asked what the unusual name meant, the manager laughed and said it was a Spanish name for a French restaurant. Actually, it could better be described as continental, and it is undeniably gourmet. "El Biz," as it is usually referred to, is certainly one of the outstanding restaurants in the San Diego area. Once again, package planners can approach its fabulous menus with gay abandon. Appetizers of lobster and artichoke hearts are a delicious way to begin, followed by a choice of hot or cold soup, and then an outstanding Caesar salad concocted tableside. From there, an entrée of quail, fish, chateaubriand, or rack of lamb, to name but a few, is guaranteed to satisfy the most discriminating taste. A fine list of California wines complements the dinner, followed by a tempting selection of dessert pastries, all adding up to delightful dining and a most pleasant evening.

If you stay more than a few nights and want a variation from El Biz and the Veranda, a short drive to the pretty little town of Rancho Bernardo will bring you to several restaurants that make pleasant dining alternatives. Monterey Jack's Prime Rib and Seafood House, just off Bernardo Center Drive, is a favorite with locals and deserves its good reputation. Fans of tempura cooking can find excellent cuisine at the Japanese Restaurant Yae in downtown Rancho Bernardo. Our own favorite is a small Italian restaurant in the Mercado Plaza opened recently by the Christafanos family. The operation is new, but the recipes are old, traditional Italian dishes prepared and seasoned with great care by the Christafanos according to your personal taste. The veal scallopini marsala and the scampi sauté are two dishes we can vouch for, never having tasted finer. The family is from New York and designed their restaurant to emulate the small, intimate establishments typical of that city. It all adds up to a delightful dining experience, and when it is time to sign on the bottom line, you will be surprised at how reasonable the evening has been.

For quick sandwiches and cold drinks, there is a small snack bar at the inn, located below the terrace. This is convenient at lunchtime for golfers between nines and tennis players fresh off the courts who don't wish to take valuable time out for formal eating.

Sea Lodge

Distances:
>   From Los Angeles—90 miles; allow 2 hours
>   From downtown San Diego—14 miles; allow ½ hour

Features:
>   A large inn facing directly onto a wide, smooth beach; tennis is free
>   on two courts; located in a quiet area, with generally moderate
>   temperatures, but lots of sunshine

Activities:
>   All ocean and beach activities, including safe swimming, surfing,
>   surf fishing, and ideal jogging; heated swimming pool, tennis
>   and golf nearby, shopping in La Jolla (pronounced La Hoya),
>   and visiting museums and other institutions in the area

Seasons:
>   Year-round

Rates:
> $85 to $120 for two people in summer, $75 to $100 in fall, $80 to
> $110 in winter, and $75 to $105 in spring; some rooms avail-
>   able with small kitchenettes

Address:
>   8110 Camino del Oro, La Jolla, California 92037

Phone:
>   (619) 459-8271

La Jolla's Sea Lodge

If you descend into the seaside village of La Jolla Shores from the east, where the hills rise steeply above the beach, the most prominent landmark will be the red tile roofs hugging the shoreline just at the center of the beach. This is Sea Lodge, a massive inn in an architectural style patterned after the hacienda of old Mexico. You enter it through a heavy ornamental iron gate, which opens into a big tiled courtyard filled with colorful flowers around a lovely fountain in the center. Circling the court are tiered balconies of second- and third-story galleries that lead to individual rooms. The walls are a restful terra cotta, highlighted by red tile fretwork to complement the sweep of tiled roofs.

The main feature of Sea Lodge is not the buildings, however, but the wide, smooth beach the buildings open onto as if the beach itself were a part of the architectural plan. The sand is white, clean, and slopes toward the water in a long, easy gradient that makes this one of the world's finest and safest beaches for swimming and other ocean sports.

With the hills behind and the ocean in front, the remaining two sides of Sea Lodge are flanked by a large carefully maintained public park to the north and the equally parklike setting of the famous La Jolla Beach and Tennis Club to the south. The surrounding neighborhood is a quiet, pretty section of tree-lined streets and comfortable residences, with a tiny, artistic commercial section known as The Village only a block from the lodge. Here you will find a cluster of little shops, including a small grocery that keeps long hours, a sports store, a tennis shop that will make quick string repairs, a deli that will pack lunches to take to the beach, and a quaint German restaurant that features outdoor dining in good weather—which is most of the time. There is a great deal of sunshine, and temperatures are moderate and springlike year-round, the days blemished only by an occasional winter fog that rolls in off the ocean at night but usually dissipates by late morning in time for tennis and beach activities.

Routes and Distances

On most maps, La Jolla appears to be part of San Diego, although it is actually a separate community occupying a bulge of land jutting into the ocean to the west and north of the city. Sea Lodge is at the north end of La Jolla in a section known as La Jolla Shores.

To get to Sea Lodge from the north, follow Interstate 5 to the La Jolla Village Drive exit. Stay on Village Drive to the second traffic light, then turn left on Torrey Pines Road. Proceed to the third light and go right on La Jolla Shores Drive. Go two blocks to Avenida de la Playa, which will bring you to Sea Lodge.

From the south, take I-5 to the Ardath Road exit. Follow Ardath Road, and at the second light go right on La Jolla Shores Drive for two blocks to Avenida de la Playa, then left to Sea Lodge.

When you arrive at Sea Lodge, drive down a ramp into a protected basement parking area. An elevator will take you from there to the lobby and check-in desk on the main floor.

Accommodations

Sports, shopping, and sightseeing can all be important elements of a good vacation, but there are times when a quiet, comfortable room for reading, watching television, or relaxing in elegant solitude are equally important. For that, you need a big room, nicely furnished, clean and airy, free from distractions, and with pleasant outside views—just like the ones you will find at Sea Lodge.

The rooms all have two queen beds—or the equivalent, such as a king and a twin—with a separate dressing room and bath area, a color television set, a small refrigerator, two or three comfortable lounge chairs and a card table, and more chairs and a table outside on the balcony or lanai. The only noise is the muffled roar of the surf at night, since most rooms face the ocean. With parking in the basement, an elevator from there directly to your level, and room service available at all hours, you could spend days at Sea Lodge, if solitude is what you want, and never meet another guest.

The inner courtyard and pool

All told, the lodge has 101 rooms on its three levels. Most of them are classified as standard rooms, as just described. There are also three deluxe rooms, which cost twelve dollars more per night and are distinguished primarily by their particularly fine oceanfront exposures. Finally, there are some kitchenette rooms, preferred by those with children and people on an extended stay. The kitchenettes rent for seven dollars per night more than standards, an extra fee not difficult to recoup by cooking just a meal or two. The little grocery and the deli nearby in the village are handy for obtaining the necessities for those who want to cook, and for beverages and snacks for all others.

Activities

Activities at Sea Lodge center naturally about the beach and the ocean. The building is horseshoe-shaped, with the restaurant and swimming pool area in the center and the open end facing out toward the water. You can walk out past the pool, cross a wide concrete promenade that fronts this entire section of beach, and be out on the sand. Joggers, runners, and walkers are all quick to take advantage of this wide, smooth, scenic stretch.

The beach slopes so gently here that the water is seldom more than waist-deep even fifty yards or more into the surf. For that reason, and because the shelter of a hook of land known as Alligator Head tends to produce uniform, medium-size swells and breakers with minimum undertow, this is an ideal place to practice surfing. Year-round, from first light until evening, you can usually see surfers on their boards working the waves. Undaunted in winter months, when the water temperature falls, they don wet suits and keep to their practice.

After the beach comes tennis, and after tennis, golf, with the lodge's attractive heated pool in the courtyard to come back to after the other endeavors.

For tennis players, this is premier country. The La Jolla Beach and Tennis Club next door is famous nationwide, and has long been host to top tournaments every year, with many of the players finding it convenient to stay at Sea Lodge. The lodge itself used to have three good all-weather courts of its own, but expansion of the dining room infringed on one court, so now only two are available for the full-time use of guests. Their use is free, however, so it is only necessary to sign up early at the front desk to reserve a playing time.

Two respectable, scenic eighteen-hole public golf courses are just a few miles north of the lodge between Torrey Pines Road and the ocean at the Torrey Pines Municipal Golf Course. The little Spindrift pitch-and-putt course, for sharpening up strokes, is practically next door.

It would be easy to spend a week in La Jolla just getting to know the area. Begin by asking at the front desk for a free map of La Jolla—

Sea Lodge fronts on the Pacific

they can give you one that lists all the highlights and how to get to them. Look for the coast walk off Prospect Place, for instance, just around the point to the south of the lodge, where you can follow the bluff and see important oceanscapes. There are other good walking trips to take, including whale watching at Wipeout Beach and Seal Rock. You can also stroll through the international shops area of La Jolla town, a unique row where the shops have fine ocean views and you can enjoy the commercial life and the scenery simultaneously. These are all on the map.

The renowned Scripps Oceanographic Institute, a mile to the north, has its own museum, an aquarium, and an underwater park that can be explored by scuba divers. In San Diego, only a fifteen-minute drive away, there are more natural exhibits to see at the San Diego Zoo, Sea World, and Balboa Park with its many museums.

In the summer season, from July to September, thoroughbreds race at the Del Mar Track, six miles north of the lodge off I-5. Finally, if you haven't been there before, it is an event to make the forty-minute drive to see the nightlife in the Mexican border town of Tijuana. Americans, with their money, are always welcome, and no passports or visas are required. It is, to be sure, an artificial and glittering "tourist attraction," but like so many things, an experience worth doing once.

Dining

Three dining rooms are within easy walking distance for Sea Lodge guests. First is the lodge's own restaurant, The Sala Del Mar, which serves three meals a day and provides full room service. Like the lodge, it is of Spanish design in a large open-beamed room with wrought ironwork and arched windows facing the ocean. The food is good and the prices are reasonable here, and one of its nicest features is that in warm weather it extends service to the colorful umbrella tables flanking the pool.

After the Sala Del Mar, the place to try is the Marine Room at the Beach Club next door. You get to it by a pleasant ten-minute stroll down the beach, as it too is on the ocean at the far end of the Beach Club property. (At certain times, when the weather is acting up and the tide is high, waves can come right up to the Marine Room's window. In that case, walk or drive around by road and get a window table to enjoy the excitement.) The large Marine Room is divided into two sections, with a lounge in the middle. As one of the favorite places on this part of the coast for local people who want a night out, it is usually crowded and bubbling with activity. It features beef and seafood cuisine, with prices in the same range as those at the Sala Del Mar.

The third place nearby is the little German restaurant in The

Village, called Rheinlander Hans. It is authentically furnished with European antiques in a clutter of lace, bric-a-brac, beer steins, and elk horns. Its prettiest feature is the outdoor patio dining area sheltered and shaded by big, leafy trees between the tables.

Across the street from the Rheinlander Hans, the Deli sells makings for lunch and breakfast. It claims to have a hundred brands of imported and exotic beer in stock.

In La Jolla itself, the Skyroom of the stately old Valencia Hotel offers intimate, elegant (but not inexpensive) dining, with magnificent harbor views. A block up the street, on the same side, is the Top of the Cove restaurant in an antique Victorian house. At noon, the prettiest time of day, the Top of the Cove serves a very reasonable buffet lunch. It is quite popular, so reservations are in order. For a pleasant evening experience, have dinner at the Valencia and then walk down to the Top of the Cove for a drink in its saloon-style bar.

The list of eating places in La Jolla and vicinity is nearly inexhaustible, but two other particularly worth mention are The Crab Catcher, overlooking La Jolla Canyon on Prospect Street, and a tiny place for top-notch Chinese food, called simply Miss China. It serves no liquor, but you are welcome to bring your own wine or Chinese beer from the Deli.

Singing Hills Lodge

Distances:
   From San Diego—17 miles; allow 25 minutes
   From Los Angeles—126 miles; allow 2½ hours
Features:
   A golfer's paradise, set in an ancient olive grove in a hill-ringed
      valley; close to San Diego but seems light-years away; low
      prices and pleasant surroundings prevail
Activities:
   Golf, tennis, swimming; short drive to Sea World, San Diego Zoo,
      Balboa Park, and museums
Seasons:
   Year-round
Rates:
   $47 weekdays for two people, $52 weekends; $55 to $60 for two-
      room suites for two people; larger suites are available for four
      or more
Address:
   3007 Dahesa Road, El Cajon, California 92021
Phone:
   (619) 442-3425

Singing Hills lodgings in an olive grove

How often have you heard avid golfers or tennis buffs wishing they could find a spot to get away for a few days to enjoy their sport without spending a small fortune? Singing Hills, in El Cajon, California, may be just the place to satisfy this wish. And even though it is less than half an hour from San Diego and just a little over two hours from the Los Angeles area, it has a rural setting and countrified atmosphere. Located in the pastoral Sweetwater River Valley, the Singing Hills resort sprawls tranquilly under the gray-green trees of an ancient olive grove, looking out over a rolling terrain dotted with giant oaks and sycamores and surrounded by majestic mountains.

Guests at the lodge enjoy the amenities of both a private golf course and a private tennis club at prices reasonable enough to arouse suspicion that there must be a catch; but there is none. Room rates are lower than those for many standard motels, and the excellent meals in the coffee shop and dining room are correspondingly reasonable. Greens fees at the three different eighteen-hole courses are lower than those at comparable courses, and the tennis club offers the use of its beautiful facilities for only $3.00 per person per hour or $5.50 all day.

Another nice thing about Singing Hills is that you'll have no need for a car during your stay. The eighty units of the lodge are all arranged to provide direct access to the golf course, so golfers can easily tote their own bags back and forth from the clubhouse. The dining facilities, which overlook the first tees of all three golf courses, are also just a short stroll from the rooms. Only tennis players determined to save every ounce of their energy for the courts elect to drive the short distance along Willow Road to the tennis club.

Those who don't want to spend all their time playing golf or tennis can explore the surrounding area. The world-famous San Diego Zoo, for example, is just twenty minutes away, and the fascinating Sea World only twenty-five minutes. There are countless other exciting places to visit throughout the neighboring region, including the Mexican border and the sights of Tijuana and the Baja Peninsula, which are less than half an hour away on the new freeway.

Routes and Distances

El Cajon is twelve and a half miles due east of San Diego on Interstate 8. On the western side of town, look for the El Cajon Boulevard exit. Take it, follow the boulevard just a few blocks to the Washington Street turn-off, and go right on Washington Street for 3.3 miles to the point where it jogs left and joins Dehesa Road. Take Dehesa for a steep, winding 2.2 miles to the resort. You will know when you are getting close when you see the golf courses and tennis club below in a valley to the right.

Accommodations

The guest quarters at Singing Hills are in seven contemporary buildings, ranging from one to three stories, that are arranged among the olive trees in such a way that most of the units have a view overlooking the golf course fairways. The greenery of these fairways, combined with the many lushly planted gardens and shade trees, creates the pleasant illusion that the resort is in the midst of a verdant oasis.

Three types of accommodations are available, the first and by far the most numerous of which are the very modestly priced hotel rooms. These are good-sized square bedrooms, with spacious adjoining dressing areas. Each is furnished with a double bed, a twin bed made up as a studio couch, a game table with four comfortable chairs, easy chair with a reading lamp, a large dresser, and a television set. Stall showers rather than bathtubs are standard throughout the resort. The interior dividing walls of all units are constructed of thick, simulated white adobe brick, which provides effective soundproofing. These walls are attractively decorated with hand-painted flowers and graceful tree branches.

Next in size are the two-room suites. These have living rooms outfitted with two studio couches that convert to twin beds, a separate bedroom with a queen bed, a dressing room, and a bath. These accom-

The tennis club is a short walk from the resort

modations are ideal for couples who want extra space or for those with children, but they are not a good arrangement for two couples.

The third kind of accommodation, the executive two-bedroom suites, are appropriate for a foursome traveling together. The cost to each couple is less than it would be for an individual standard room, and these units have some added attractions. They are more expensively decorated and overlook the pool as well as the golf course. Their big living rooms, excellent for entertaining or just relaxing, have attractive wet bars with built-in refrigerators and comfortable couch and coffee table arrangements in addition to the usual game ensemble, easy chair, and television of the smaller units. There are two separate bedrooms, each with a private bath, in addition to a dressing room. The floor plan of the executive suites is conducive to both comfort and privacy, which makes them very popular. Since only a few are available, you should get your request in early if these are the accommodations you want.

Activities

There are fifty-four holes of golf at Singing Hills, in what many consider one of the prettiest layouts in the area—and, since being completely rebuilt in 1981, one of the more challenging. A series of floods between 1978 and 1980 devastated the then well-known but relatively unexciting course, bringing Singing Hills to a standstill. The owners decided to take the opportunity to completely redesign and upgrade the course and hired Ted Robinson, one of the country's three top golf course architects, to do the job. Robinson was struck by the natural beauty of the valley and, at a cost of some three million dollars, completely transformed the old layout to take advantage of the surroundings. He also installed a modern flood control system to prevent any more untoward events.

What was once a flat course with its difficulties primarily due to distance is now marked by undulating greens, six new lakes, and scientifically and artistically designed bunkers and fairways that place a premium on shot placement so that, according to Robinson, "you have to think your way around the course," as well as be able to hit a long ball.

The new course is three separate eighteens, all of which start at the clubhouse and fan out across the valley. To the left, facing out from the clubhouse, is the Oak Glen course, 6100 yards, par-seventy-one, rated 68.8. In the middle is the Willow Glen course, 6573 yards, par-seventy-two, rated 71.4. To the far right, running close to the swimming pool and guest lodges, is the Pine Glen executive course, 2276 yards at par-fifty-four.

The two long courses are particularly scenic from the profusion of old oaks and sycamores and natural rock outcrops the architect was careful to preserve, and the little executive course has a lovely setting among the trees of the ancient olive grove.

The head professional at Singing Hills is Tom Addis III, well known in Southern California and president of the Southern California section of the PGA in 1982. He has a brand-new, 2800-square-foot pro shop, well stocked with everything a golfer might need, and next to the shop there are extensive practice facilities, including a regular putting green, a second green surrounded by traps to practice blasting out, and a driving range for both long shots and approach shots.

All lodge guests are also welcome to use the Singing Hills Tennis Club facility located on Willow Glen Drive, a quarter-mile from the resort itself. This is a private club maintained by dues-paying members, so lodge guests are charged nominally on a daily basis. It has eleven top-quality, individually fenced and screened, hard-surface courts with good night lighting. The clubhouse houses a complete pro shop. Private lessons and group clinics for adult and junior players are available from the full-time teaching staff.

Golf and tennis together constitute 98 percent of the activities at Singing Hills, but the pretty little swimming pool gets some attention, and there are always a few joggers using the wide shoulders on the surrounding roads—or the cart paths around the courses if they get up early enough. The wide shoulders are fine for bicycling, too, if you

There are fifty-four holes of golf to play at Singing Hills

bring your own bicycle; none is available on the premises.

Dining

Guests staying at Singing Hills Lodge usually have all their meals in the clubhouse and find it a pleasant way to enjoy the friendly ambience of this country club setting.

The Vista Room, which is the club's coffee shop, opens every morning at 6:30 A.M.and in no time is bustling with golfers eager to get out on the course for an early start. People come in a steady stream from then on, until the coffee shop closes at 4:00 P.M. At noon, the luncheon menus are brought out, and the service switches from breakfast to sandwiches and salads, which are often served with a cold beer, as the early bird golfers come in after finishing their game and the late starters stop off between nines.

In the evening the activity moves to the Cesta Room, which is more elegant but has the same friendly, informal atmosphere found elsewhere at the resort. As the Spanish name suggests, baskets are the decorating motif, and baskets of all sizes and shapes cover all the walls except for one long window wall, which provides a pleasant view of rolling lawn and colorful flower beds.

There is a copy of the dinner menu in each room, so you can consider the possibilities in advance. A glance at it confirms the reasonableness of the prices here. There is a good selection of seafood and charcoal broiled steaks, along with such club specialties as barbecued ribs, pork chops, fried chicken, and chicken cordon bleu. The service and preparation of food in the Cesta Room is every bit as appealing as the prices.

For those who care to linger, a piano bar is located directly adjacent to the dining room. The pianist will usually play old tunes on request, and you can listen quietly or get up and keep time to the music on a small dance floor.

For those who come to Singing Hills for an extended stay and want some variety, there are several good places for dinner in El Cajon. Ask at the desk for directions to Pancho Villa's, if you like Mexican food, or to Lorenzo's for Italian food or steaks. The Top Shelf also serves excellent steaks, and if fresh fish broiled on an open pit of mesquite charcoal sounds enticing, try the San Lucos Fish House.

Half Moon Inn

Distances:

From downtown San Diego—4 miles; allow 15 minutes

From Los Angeles—130 miles; allow 2½ hours

Features:

Polynesian-style inn in a verdant, tropical, harborfront setting, close to San Diego's many attractions

Activities:

Use of swimming pool, hot spa and marina on premises; Sea World, San Diego Zoo, Old Town, historic exhibits, ocean beaches, and museums, nearby

Seasons:

Inn operates year-round; weather is generally warm and sunny except in May and June, when morning fog is common

Rates:

$90 for a room for two people at peak season (July to August); off-season prices start at $59

Address:

2303 Shelter Island Drive, San Diego, California 92106

Phone:

(619) 224-3411; toll free in California (800) 532-3737; toll free outside California (800) 854-2900

Half Moon Inn's Polynesian-style rooms on the yacht harbor

Half Moon Inn is a little different from most resorts. Except for the swimming pool, it has no athletic facilities or any of the usual organized diversions, but these are unnecessary because its distinction is an enviable location, centrally situated, with easy access to everything in the extraordinarily well-endowed San Diego area. Yet, close as it is to the pleasures of city life, the resort is outside the downtown section and away from traffic and noise.

The inn is a low, rambling, Polynesian-style building appropriately placed in a lush garden setting on a narrow neck of land called Shelter Island—which is not really an island at all, but a T-shaped landfill that juts into San Diego Bay.

The narrowness of the "island" gives most of the inn's rooms marine views, either to the bay in front or over the big, protected yacht harbor on the other side. A marine atmosphere pervades the entire surrounding area. Shelter Island Drive, on which you approach the inn, is lined on both sides for its whole length by yacht brokers, ship repair yards, boat builders, and chandleries, all interspersed with little waterfront restaurants, bars, and moorage docks. Across on the bay side, at the head of the T, is the North Island Naval Base, and in the deepwater channel between the two a constant parade of naval traffic, commercial fishermen, and pleasure craft move in and out only a few hundred yards from the inn.

People come to Half Moon Inn primarily because they like the combination of maritime excitement and a cosmopolitan atmosphere, but also to use it as a comfortable and convenient place to head-quarter while they tour and explore this unique southwesternmost corner of the United States. Once they learn the road pattern, which is simplicity itself, they find Shelter Island to be an ideal hub from which to visit the abundant local attractions. Shelter Island Drive leads directly to Harbor Drive, which in turn takes less than fifteen minutes to make a scenic circuit around the harbor into downtown. Shelter Island Drive also takes you to Rosecrans, which leads straight into Old Town, only ten minutes away. Or, by following Rosecrans just a few blocks and turning left on Nimitz, you have a straight shot to the network of freeways that connects with all the outlying areas, Mission Bay, Sea World, and the ocean beaches.

This whole area is rich with history, so there is much to see. It was the first place on the West Coast ever glimpsed by a European when the Portuguese navigtor Cabrillo landed his little ship at Point Loma. It was also the site for the first of the chain of missions built by the Spanish explorer-priests who came to discover California on foot. These events and many more are recorded in a multitude of monuments and old buildings that still stand, and in the many museums and parks which together have made San Diego a major at-traction for tourists and visitors from all over the world.

All this is augmented, of course, by the generally fine and reliable weather for which the area is also well known, by the long list of in-teresting places to eat and drink in the vicinity, and by the comfort and convenience of this particular inn.

Routes and Distances

From downtown San Diego, the shortest route to the inn is to take Harbor Drive and follow the waterfront all the way around San Diego Bay, past Harbor Island, to Shelter Island Drive. Turn left on the drive to its end, where you will see the unmistakable swooping roof of Half Moon Inn.

From the north, come in on any of the southbound freeways, In-terstate 5, Interstate 15, or California 163, until you intersect the east-west freeway, Interstate 8. Exit west on I-8 and follow it to its end at Nimitz Boulevard. Turn left on Nimitz for two miles to Rosecrans Street, and turn right there for about three-tenths of a mile to the prominent Shelter Island Drive sign. As above, follow the drive to its end and the inn.

Accommodations

The setting of the inn assures that virtually all of its 136 rooms

The Shelter Island yacht basin from the inn's balcony

have interesting views. Those that don't look out to the harbor with its masses of sailboats and other craft, or over the bay to North Island and downtown San Diego, have sliding glass doors that open onto the swimming pool in the middle of the lush tropical garden.

The price range of the regular rooms is based in large part on the quality of the view afforded by each, because in other respects they are nearly identical. All are roomy and tastefully decorated, with muted colors in the rugs and furnishings brightly accented by the drapes and bedspreads. Most of these rooms are furnished with two queen-size beds, although a few have kings. A large dressing room and a bath with twin sinks add to the convenience of the arrangement.

The rooms are all placed in closely knit two-story bungalows on both sides of the central swimming pool and courtyard, where they allow easy access to the restaurant, front office, pool, and spa. The standard rooms are in the centers of these buildings, with the corner locations given over to roomy suites that have window exposures on two sides. These suites have full-sized but lightly equipped kitchens, separate bedrooms, and a comfortable living–dining room with couches, chairs, and tables. Decks open from both their living areas and bedrooms. These are a good choice for those who want plenty of space and facilities for preparing their own breakfasts and lunches. The living room couch converts into a double bed, and there is direct access from either the bedroom or living room into the dressing room–bath area, so the suites also are suitable for two couples who want to travel together and share quarters.

Activities

The most pressing problem for visitors to San Diego is deciding among the dozens of options to make the best use of their time. Our suggestions, in rough order of preference, are as follows: a half-day at Sea World, a half-day at the zoo, a couple of hours in Old Town, a trip out to the Cabrillo National Monument at the end of Point Loma, another half-day devoted to the museums in Balboa Park, and finally, the fifty-two-mile scenic drive, which is well marked on a free Visitor's Bureau map available from the concierge at the inn.

The only trouble with such a program is that it doesn't leave a great deal of time to laze around the inn's pretty swimming pool, or for trips to the beach, cruising San Diego Harbor, driving down to Mexico, deep-sea fishing, or sailing on the bay. It comes down to how much time is available and what your preferences are, with the only sure thing being that San Diego offers a lengthy smorgasbord of choices. You may well decide while you are here to solve the problem

Trained killer whales at nearby Sea World

by coming back as soon as possible.

In any event, Half Moon Inn is a fine place to start out from. Sea World, for instance, is no more than fifteen minutes away, and those who have not watched the trained whales, seals, and dolphins owe it to themselves to make this pilgrimage and discover the stunning intelligence and hilarious entertainment provided by these remarkable animals.

The San Diego Zoo in Balboa Park, also only fifteen minutes from the inn, has long been recognized as one of the best zoos in the world. The half-day visit we suggest is the absolute minimum here.

Old Town San Diego is even closer than the park. Go back out Rosecrans Street the way you came in and follow it to its end at Old Town, where the American flag was first raised over California in 1846. The whole six-block area of historic buildings, the reconstructed original plaza, museums, shops, and restaurants is closed to automobiles. It is a colorful place for a leisurely stroll and lunch in one of the outdoor cafés.

Another short trip is the drive to the tip of Point Loma. Go west on Rosecrans to where it intersects Catalina Boulevard, then follow the boulevard along the spine of Point Loma to the Cabrillo National Monument at its tip. A Park Service exhibit at the monument site describes early Portuguese explorations. The point's high headland has a magnificent view of San Diego Bay, North Island, the city on the far shore, and on a clear day, Mexico in the distance.

Most of San Diego's many museums are clustered handily in Balboa Park near the zoo, making it possible to combine all the museums in one trip. Of particular interest are the Museum of Man, the Aero-Space Museum, and the Natural History Museum. There are six more museums in the park and a half-dozen more in the neighborhood.

A popular diversion is to leave the automobile behind and tour the harbor by boat. Yachts leave three times a day from nearby Harbor Island on two-hour cruises around the shore of North Island and along the city waterfront. There is no better way to see and appreciate the essence of San Diego than with a crew that points out the sights, and serves cocktails, too, on order.

Those who prefer to do it on their own can rent sailboats at Harbors Sailboats, also on Harbor Island. Rentals are by the hour, the day, or the week, with a selection of boats ranging from fourteen-foot Capris to thirty-nine-foot Santanas.

Between Shelter Island and Harbor Island are moorages for rows of large, seagoing charter boats. Sport fishermen can stroll along the docks here shopping for a boat and skipper to take them out for as long and as far as they want to go: everything from half-day trips off Point Loma to week-long cruises down the Baja Peninsula. Albacore tuna, skipjack, yellowtail, sea bass, and a score of other game fish are caught in these waters.

The Del Mar Racetrack, open during the summer, is an easy drive on the freeway from Shelter Island, and so offers yet another diversion for those staying at Half Moon Inn.

What else is there to do after all this? In the evenings or early mornings, you can jog or walk out to the end of Shelter Island or around the head of the bay to the Yacht Club. For exercise, and for a chance to see a display of thousands of colorful boats in their moorages, this flat, scenic terrain is ideal.

Dining

The Half Moon's restaurant, Humphrey's, is one of the more popular in the San Diego area and is located just a short stroll through the garden from your room. Built on pilings at the water's edge, it offers views across the harbor and yacht basin toward Point Loma.

Several years ago, when the "Bogie" cult was going strong, the restaurant was completely redesigned to reflect the ambience of Casablanca, circa 1942. Brass ceiling fans with wide blades, high-back rattan furniture, and verdant tropical plants all contribute to a contemporary California homage to the classic Bogart-Bergman film. Due partly to its convenient location and partly to its attractive atmosphere, Humphrey's is a popular meeting place at lunchtime for local people, who flock in and keep the place buzzing with activity.

The luncheon goings-on barely foreshadow what happens later in the lounge, Humphrey's Pump, when the "happy hour" starts at 4:30. Happy hours are particularly popular in the San Diego area, where many lounges put out elaborate spreads of hors d'oeuvres and serve drinks at reduced prices. Each night of the week Humphrey's carries out this tradition with a different theme: on Tuesdays, for example mai tais, piña coladas, and daiquiris are teamed with fried shrimp, wontons, and sweet-and-sour pork; on Fridays, premium California wines are served by the glass along with cold broiled shrimp. Similar specialties are offered throughout the week, and there is always lively music at the piano bar.

When it is time to move into the restaurant for dinner, you may be seated indoors or outside on the deck overlooking the harbor. Maine lobster, flown in daily, is the dinner specialty and you can choose your own from a big tank in the lobby or have the lobster pot dinner, which includes clams, mussels, and half a Dungeness crab along with the lobster. If you don't like lobster, or don't want to pay so dearly, there are also king crab legs, veal Oscar, prime rib, steak, and plenty of other well-prepared choices.

The San Diego area has a large number of interesting restaurants to try, and the concierge at the inn will provide information about them and make reservations. A good place to start is Old Town, where several restaurants feature traditional Mexican and early California food served in outdoor gardens—Casa de Bandini and Casa de Pico are both excellent. Lino's offers good northern Italian cooking.

Anthony's Star of the Sea Room and Mr. A's, both downtown, are elegant restaurants offering continental cuisine. Ten Downing, far less formal but good fun, is a very English place where "wenches" serve fish and chips and kidney pies on pewter ware.

Tom Ham's Lighthouse Restaurant on Harbor Island in a maritime museum with a bayside view, is a traditional favorite. So is the *Reuben E. Lee,* a Mississippi stern-wheeler converted into a restaurant that serves good seafood and of course has fine harbor views.

Hotel del Coronado

Distances:
> From downtown San Diego—15 to 20 minutes across the toll bridge
> From Los Angeles—130 miles; allow 2½ to 3 hours

Features:
> One of America's largest and best loved seaside resorts, now augmented with a full array of modern recreational equipment

Activities:
> Ocean swimming, sunning and strolling on wide beach, swimming in heated pool, tennis, health spa, golf nearby; exploring all of San Diego's many attractions

Seasons:
> Year-round

Rates:
> Rooms from $68 to $175 for two people, depending on view and location; suites available from $180

Address:
> 1500 Orange Avenue, Coronado, California 92118

Phone:
> (619) 435-6611

The Hotel del Coronado—a grande dame built in the 1800s

One compelling reason for coming to the Hotel del Coronado is just to see the Hotel del Coronado. It is probably the finest remaining example of the huge, elegant, ornate, frame seaside resort hotels built in America during the later part of the 1800s. Today it is registered as a national Historic Landmark and is invariably included on every list of the country's top resort hotels.

The hotel is five stories high, containing 366 rooms in the massive original section, adorned with fantastic cupolas and towers and Victorian gingerbread woodwork. It is hard to believe the entire structure was built in one year by artisans working from sketchy drawings at a time when skilled labor had to be brought all the way from San Francisco.

A beautiful setting on the ocean, ideal weather, and its air of opulence quickly attracted socially prominent people from all over the world, establishing "The Del's" success from the very beginning. Since then, the number of rooms has been nearly doubled with the addition of two annexes known as the Tower and the Poolside Buildings. The saltwater swimming pool that old-timers remember has been replaced by a big, new, heated freshwater pool, and the old billiard rooms replaced by a health spa and exercise rooms. A row of fine tennis courts has been built, and all the rooms have been periodically modernized and redecorated to keep up with the times.

The Del has thus managed to merge its old-time elegance with up-to-date amenities in a way that assures and continually enhances its reputation and popularity. This is evident at almost any time of any day just from the number of people milling through the cavernous lobby, up and down the many halls and passages, and around the pretty central courtyard. The crowds of tourists and vacationers are augmented by a procession of weddings and other social events. The Del is also a favored place for professional meetings and symposia, and their participants, identifiable by the time-honored name tags on the lapel, contribute to the constant whirl of activity.

In a nutshell, The Del fills the enviable role among hotels of being all things to all people—a fancy oceanfront resort, a convention center, a community social center, a business stopover, and just a nice place to meet friends for lunch. It does them all and does them well.

Routes and Distances

Get on Interstate 5 at San Diego and follow it south out of the city to the California 75–Coronado Bridge exit. The exit puts you immediately onto the graceful bridge that crosses the bay to Coronado, built very high to permit the largest naval vessels to proceed without interference.

At the Coronado end of the bridge a tollbooth collects $1.20 for the round trip. Continue to follow Highway 75 in a curving half-circle into the village of Coronado. On the south side of the village, you will see the unmistakable red-roofed towers of the hotel. Park temporarily at the check-in area—you will need the help of an employee to find your room and take the luggage in. The employee will also direct you to a permanent parking space and explain the one-time $4.00 parking charge for guests' cars.

Accommodations

About half of The Del's seven hundred rooms are modern hotel-style, located in the two new buildings, with the balance in the original grand old structure. The latter, five stories tall, is built in a square with rooms on all four sides enclosing a garden courtyard in the center. The design results in a wide variety of different views and outlooks, and moreover, according to the bellman who carried our luggage inside, no two of the old building's rooms are alike; this is, of course, part of the hotel's charm.

If you stay in the old part, which many feel is necessary to really experience The Del, the price you pay depends entirely on the room size and view, and whether it has a balcony or not. The "standard" are the least expensive rooms. They are quite small, furnished with two twin beds, and generally have a minimal view on the side toward

Guests gather at the gazebo in the inner courtyard

the town of Coronado. The "medium" room is larger, but on a low level, looking over the courtyard. "Deluxe" rooms have either an oceanfront or bay view or are high on the courtyard, but have no balconies. At the top of the line, excluding suites, are the large "lanai" rooms, with ocean or bay views, comfortable sitting areas, and usually with a balcony—some with gaily colored awnings. In most of these rooms, except the standards, some choice of beds is available: a king, two queens, doubles, or twins.

The original hotel rooms do not have the separate dressing areas, modern baths with double sinks, and similar conveniences enjoyed by the new complex, but any such sacrifices are more than made up for, many people agree, by the graceful charm of these century-old quarters. A typical room is papered in a delicate, old-fashioned, pale yellow or blue, and the woodwork is painted white, as are the headboards, dressers, desks, and wicker chairs, creating a bright and airy effect. The drapes, rugs, and bedspreads are coordinated in a contrasting sunny color.

In the newer buildings, the rooms are also designated "standard" to "lanai," and priced according to the same factors of view, size, and location. On the whole, these rooms are somewhat larger, are priced a little higher, and have small dressing rooms and sitting areas. They are also less diverse than those in the old building, but many have fine locations right on the beach or opening onto one of the two swimming pools. This, together with the modern fixtures and other up-to-date touches, tips the balance in their favor for some guests.

Activities

A thorough exploration of the hotel and grounds is always the first order of business, and it takes a few hours of prowling the halls, lobbies, and walkways inside and out to get oriented in this magnificent structure. The lower hallways take considerable extra time because they are lined with framed newspaper accounts and photographs of historic events since the hotel's founding, including visits by princes, presidents, and famous personalities who all have become part of the hotel's legend. One hall is devoted to exhibits of memorabilia: tools used during construction, 1800s office equipment, original room furnishings, and many more old photographs of the early days. The lobbies and lounges are copiously furnished with beautiful antiques that take more time to inspect, many pieces having histories of their own. There is so much about the hotel to explain, in fact, that a self-guided tape-recorded tour is available, and can be checked out at the front desk. You sling the machine over your shoulder, put on the earphones, and the tape guides you around the premises, explaining everything as you go.

The main swimming pool is scaled in proportion to the hotel. It is four times the size of the usual hotel pool and is always a central attraction, not only for the swimmers and sunbathers, but also because it is bordered on three sides by elevated terraces lined with umbrella tables and served by a bar in a towerlike gazebo at one corner. Down below, on the pool deck, is a deli for light snacks and an attendant with towels and miscellaneous pool supplies, so it is perfectly possible to spend the whole day around the pool—which is exactly what a great many guest are content to do.

The original attraction that caused the hotel to be built in this spot in the first place is the beach—one of California's finest—which all the best rooms look out upon. It is indeed a magnificent sight: wide, silver-colored, and gently sloping, making it ideal for swimming, surfing, jogging, walking, and picnicking.

In a row between the hotel and the beach, behind protective windscreens, are seven hard-surfaced tennis courts, individually fenced and lighted at night. The reservations necessary for play can be made in the small tennis shop facing the courts. A fee of $12 per court hour is charged for use—stiff, but apparently no deterrent, as the courts are always busy.

Few people come to The Del just to play golf, but for anyone addicted to the sport, the eighteen-hole Coronado Municipal course is

Tennis tournaments in an old-world setting

only a few minutes' drive from the hotel. Or, for sailors, it is a short walk to the Glorietta Marina, located on a bayside dock behind the old Del Coronado boathouse, where boats can be rented. On a good day, with a bit of breeze, this is a pleasant way to explore the San Diego environs. Seventeen- to twenty-two-foot sailboats and some outboards are available, priced from $9 to $15 per hour.

Back at the hotel, in accord with the modern trend toward physical fitness, you will find two identical but separate health spas for men and for women on the lower level by the tennis shop. Each has a mirrored work-out room full of weights, equipment, and a big 102-degree hot spa almost the size of a miniature swimming pool. Off the spas are steam rooms and sunlamp rooms, and massages are available by appointment. Attendants are on duty in each spa to help patrons take advantage of the equipment, set up exercise schedules, supply towels and lockers, and collect the $5 charge for use of the spa.

Dining

One cannot help being struck by the size and opulence of the grand old dining room opening off of the hotel's main lobby. The

Crown Room has scarcely changed since it was built almost a century ago. Its arched, thirty-one-foot ceiling is natural-finish sugar pine fitted together with pegs, nary a nail, with a unique support system that requires no interior posts or columns. The light fixtures hanging from this extraordinary ceiling are huge, crown-shaped chandeliers, world-famous in their own right. This elegant dining room overlooking the ocean can easily seat a thousand people, and has been host to a parade of notables, including presidents and royalty—in fact, it was at The Del that England's Edward met the woman for whom he later renounced his throne.

A second dining room is The Prince of Wales Grille on the hotel's lower level, commemorating an earlier 1920 visit when Edward came to the hotel as a young prince. Its decor and atmosphere are quite different from those in the grandiose Crown Room. It, too, is elegant, but small, intimate, and dimly lit, with a low ceiling, and high-back booths and furniture upholstered in Victoria red.

Downstairs in a basement cavern, The Del Deli provides simple fare, cafeteria style, for breakfast and lunch. Hot croissants with marmalade and coffee, sandwiches, and beer and wine are available at any time in a charming alcove created by chopping access tunnels through four-foot-thick concrete walls into what were once the hotel's water cisterns.

There is also a branch of The Deli by the main swimming pool for the convenience of sunbathers and swimmers, but by far the most popular place for lunch is the outdoor Oceanside Terrace, which enjoys a full view of the tennis courts and the pool, as well as the sea and beach.

The Crown Room serves all three meals, with the menu for each posted daily in the lobby just outside its entrance. When the dinner hour arrives it is time to dress up. A table d'hôte dinner with different entrées every day includes soup, salad, dessert, and beverages. There is also a selection of à la carte dishes.

In the Prince of Wales Grille, everything is à la carte, and most dishes are prepared tableside. A wide selection of entrées and an excellent wine list make this an especially pleasurable place to dine. Since it is limited in size and the staff likes to give the guests attentive individual service, reservations are desirable. Reservations are unnecessary in the Crown Room, since the space is virtually unlimited.

If you should tire of The Del's dinners, or want a less formal setting, the Chart House 1887 Restaurant is kitty-corner across the street from the hotel in the picturesque old boathouse on the bay. This restaurant is a part of a respected chain operation and serves steaks, prime rib, and seafood at relatively moderate prices. The atmosphere is relaxed and the view superb.

Checklist

House
House key
Babysitter and dog-sitter
    arranged
Doors and windows locked
Furnace turned down
Water and electric lights
    turned off
Neighbor to take in mail and
    newspapers arranged

Packing
Casual clothes
Dinner clothes
Walking shoes
Bathing suits and robes
Toilet articles

Personal
Money and checkbook
Glasses and sunglasses
Reservation confirmations
Camera and film

Refreshments
Thermos of coffee
Breakfast ingredients
Beverages
Snacks

Sports Equipment
Binoculars
Bicycles
Tennis gear
Golf gear
Fishing tackle
Clamming equipment
Rain gear
Skiing gear
Rucksack

Auto
Extra set of car keys
Chains (in winter)
Full gas tank

Special Desert Gear
Gallon jug of drinking
    water
Radiator coolant
Extra fan belt
Sun hat
Sun block lotion
First-aid kit
Snake-bite kit

Other Books from Pacific Search Press

Minnie Rose Lovgreen's Recipe for Raising Chickens
    by Minnie Rose Lovgreen
Mushrooms 'n Bean Sprouts: A First Step for Would-be Vegetarians
    by Norma M. MacRae, R.D.
My Secret Cookbook by Paula Simmons
The Natural Fast Food Cookbook by Gail L. Worstman
The Natural Fruit Cookbook by Gail L. Worstman
The Northwest Adventure Guide by Pacific Search Press
The Pike Place Market: People, Politics, and Produce
    by Alice Shorett and Murray Morgan
Rhubarb Renaissance: A Cookbook by Ann Saling
The River Pioneers: Early Days on Grays Harbor by Edwin Van Syckle
Roots & Tubers: A Vegetable Cookbook by Kyle D. Fulwiler
The Salmon Cookbook by Jerry Dennon
Seattle Photography by David Barnes
Sleek & Savage: North America's Weasel Family by Delphine Haley
Spinning and Weaving with Wool by Paula Simmons
Starchild & Holahan's Seafood Cookbook
    by Adam Starchild and James Holahan
They Tried to Cut It All by Edwin Van Syckle
Two Crows Came by Jonni Dolan
Warm & Tasty: The Wood Heat Stove Cookbook by Margaret Byrd Adams
The White-Water River Book: A Guide to Techniques, Equipment, Camping,
    and Safety by Ron Watters/Robert Winslow, photography
The Whole Grain Bake Book by Gail L. Worstman
Wild Mushroom Recipes by Puget Sound Mycological Society
Wild Shrubs: Finding and Growing Your Own by Joy Spurr
The Zucchini Cookbook by Paula Simmons